HOTEL AND CATERING LAW

HOTEL AND CATERING LAW

An Outline of the Law
Relating to Hotels, Guest Houses,
Restaurants and Other
Catering Businesses

SEVENTH EDITION

by

FRANK J. BULL
B.Com., F.C.I.S., Hon.F.H.C.I.M.A.

and

JOHN D. G. HOOPER
Barrister, of Lincoln's Inn

Approved by the Hotel, Catering and Institutional Management Association as a text book for use in preparation for the M.H.C.I.M.A. and National Diploma Examinations.

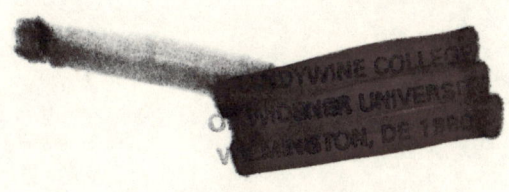

BARRIE & JENKINS
COMMUNICA - EUROPA

©Frank J. Bull and John D. G. Hooper 1979

First published by the Practical Press 1953

Second Edition 1962
Third Edition 1964
Fourth Edition 1968
published by
Barrie and Rockliff (Barrie Books Ltd.)
Fifth Edition 1970
Sixth Edition 1975
Seventh Edition 1979
published by
Barrie & Jenkins Ltd.
24 Highbury Crescent, London N5 1RX
ISBN 0 214 20069 8

First to Fifth Editions by
Frank J. Bull and Colin Richardson

All rights reserved
No part of this publication may be reproduced in any form or by any means without prior permission of Barrie & Jenkins Ltd.

Printed in Great Britain by
Clarke, Doble & Brendon Ltd.,
Plymouth and London

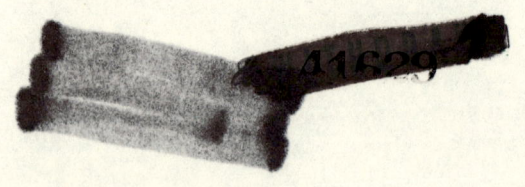

KD
2517
.H6
B8
1979

CONTENTS

	PAGE
Authors' Preface	9
Introduction	11

GUESTS and CUSTOMERS

1	The Guest at an Hotel	15
2	Where the Hotel Proprietors Act does not apply	21
3	Hotel Bookings	24
4	Guests in Residence	29
5	Guests and Customers—generally	34

THE STAFF

6	Engagement, Employment and Dismissal	41
7	Employer's other Statutory Obligations	59

FOOD

8	The Law affecting Caterers	71

THE SALE OF LIQUOR

9	The Licensing System—England and Wales	79
10	The Conduct of Licensed Premises—England and Wales	92
11	The Scottish Licensing System	103
12	The Conduct of Licensed Premises—Scotland	108
13	Registered Clubs	113

ANCILLARY SERVICES

14	Various Licences	117

THE BUSINESS

15	Obligations of the Proprietor	121

Glossary of Legal Terms	137
Appendix I—Hotel Proprietors Act 1956	141
II—Immigration (Hotel Records) Order 1972	144
III—Interpretation of a Wages Order	146
Index	147

AUTHORS' PREFACE TO SEVENTH EDITION

The year 1978 marks the Silver Jubilee of 'Hotel and Catering Law', which was first published at a time when the Hotel and Catering Institute—now the Hotel Catering and Institutional Management Association—was planning courses and examinations for managerial and other staff. Both authors were concerned in these developments.

In 1953 the industry itself was having to grapple with new problems which made some pre-war practices and legislation out-of-date. Wages regulation orders had come into force a few years earlier but were not readily absorbed by the different types of business involved, most having operating conditions to which similar provisions had not previously been applied. Proprietors of unlicensed hotels, then more numerous than now, were so concerned at the possible effects that they were instrumental in having an Inquiry by the Catering Wages Commission to consider their point of view. The commission supported them and the Unlicensed Residential Establishment Wages Board ceased to function.

Hotels providing parking and garage facilities for motorists were discovering that the old Innkeepers Liability Act 1863 did not protect them from claims for lost vehicles, and this was one of the factors which led to its repeal by the Hotel Proprietors Act of 1956.

Licensing law had, for a long time, been regarded as antiquated and although efforts to change it can be traced back to the 1930s, it was such a sensitive subject that no Government would tackle it until a Bill introduced in 1960 became the Licensing Act 1961, after months of debate, later to be consolidated in the current 1964 Act. Scotland has changed its licensing laws in two stages, first in 1962 and again in 1976.

These were some of the issues of twenty-five years ago. More recently, the law relating to employment has been drastically amended, some provisions not being in operation when the sixth edition was published. Substantial revision has therefore been necessary.

Among other changes made this time are the following:

(1) For reasons given in the Introduction, the law concerning the reception of guests is now explained in relation to hotels and hotel proprietors instead of, as formerly, to inns and innkeepers.

(2) Publicity has recently been given to reports by wages inspectors that some employers do not understand the full implications of wages orders and the Department of Employment is understood to be considering simplification. In the meantime, an appendix has been added to help in this direction.

(3) Consumer protection as currently applied to this industry now requires price displays at hotels and guest houses; this is one development of a voluntary code of booking practice designed to ensure that potential guests are fully informed before they enter into a contract. Similar requirements could apply to restaurants.

F.J.B., J.D.G.H.

INTRODUCTION

The provision of overnight accommodation and refreshment for travellers has long been the traditional role of the innkeeper, and the customs which have come to be accepted over many centuries as the basis for the relationship between host and guest still have the force of law with some modifications. The obligations and rights of innkeepers have been established as the result of decisions made by the courts, with the intervention of Parliament on two occasions in the nineteenth century to protect innkeepers against unscrupulous travellers.

A new dimension was given to this type of business by French citizens who settled in this country at the time of the revolution nearly two hundred years ago. They included some experts in the culinary arts with an appreciation of wine. Words such as 'hotel', 'cuisine' and 'menu' were added to the English vocabulary and numerous dishes continue to bear French names. The high standards introduced caught the public imagination and thereafter most new enterprises reflected a preference for the description 'hotel' where sleeping accommodation was offered, while meals were served in a 'restaurant' or light refreshments in a 'café'.

English law, however, was still concerned with inns and innkeepers, even after the Hotel Proprietors Act 1956 had confirmed that the same provisions also applied to hotels where the proprietor 'held out' that he was willing to accept all respectable travellers without picking and choosing. Most hotels are conducted on this basis, but some are not, and this situation makes it necessary to distinguish between them.

As an appropriate description has considerable significance to the public, and particularly tourists, some standardisation is desirable and the authors offer the following suggestions:

(1) The words 'hotel' or 'inn' should be used only for residential premises where the Act applies.

(2) Other residential premises where the proprietor does not provide the services or accept the obligations of an hotel proprietor should use some alternative description such as 'private hotel', 'guest house' or 'boarding house'.

(3) Non-residential premises cannot properly be called 'hotels'.

THE GUEST

THE GUEST AT AN HOTEL

The Hotel Proprietors Act 1956 defines an hotel in the following terms: 'an establishment held out by the proprietor as offering food, drink and, if so required, sleeping accommodation, without special contract, to any traveller presenting himself who appears able and willing to pay a reasonable sum for the services and facilities provided and who is in a fit state to be received.'

Where the word 'hotel' or 'inn' is part of the name, there might be a presumption that the Act would apply. but in practice there are exceptions. Some businesses retain the word 'hotel' though they have become non-residential, and others may limit the supply of food to breakfast. Any question which might arise can only be determined by the way the hotel or inn is conducted by the proprietor.

Who is a Traveller?

In cases brought before the courts, a wide interpretation has been given to the word 'traveller' so as to bring within this description anyone on a journey however short. The wise course for the proprietor is to regard all callers as travellers unless he has reason to believe otherwise.

A traveller must be respectable and able to pay, and the courts have allowed the proprietor some discretion to refuse service or accommodation on the general principle that he is entitled to have regard to good order and decency in running his business. Guests who arrive in a drunken state or who behave offensively may clearly be refused, as may anyone who by reason of his behaviour becomes unacceptable to other guests. In one case, a bookmaker who annoyed other guests by pestering them to place bets with him was held to have been reasonably refused accommodation when presenting himself on a second occasion.

The proprietor must take care not to discriminate on grounds of race or sex; if anyone brought an action against him, he would have to prove that he had acted reasonably in the circumstances.

Provision of Food and Drink

A traveller has the right to be provided with food and drink irrespective of the time of his arrival. His demands must be reasonable and consistent with the services normally available; for example, he cannot expect a hot meal at other than the usual times. If the proprietor can offer some food, he will be fulfilling his duty; if he cannot, the test would be whether he has acted reasonably in the circumstances. For example, the unexpected arrival of several travellers on a Saturday night or Sunday could justify a refusal if the only food available was needed for residents and staff.

The size and location of an hotel would have a bearing on the reception of parties, and if it was on a coach route, any notice exhibited might indicate that coach parties would be accepted by prior arrangement.

The reference to drink does not necessarily imply alcoholic liquor, as an unlicensed hotel can be within scope of the Act.

Provision of Accommodation

An hotel proprietor is obliged to receive all respectable travellers and provide accommodation for them if he has it available. This obligation is concerned with bedrooms and does not require some other room, e.g. a lounge, to be offered if all bedrooms are occupied.

The traveller's right to be received arises at the time he presents himself without special contract, that is without prior booking. The proprietor is entitled to request payment in advance, and his allocation of a room will not confer any right to retain it for an indefinite period. The proprietor may, if he finds it expedient, change the allocation at a later date and if the guest remains as a boarder or lodger he may lose his right as a traveller when the proprietor could, if he wished, give him notice to leave.

Responsibility for Guests' Property

The obligation to receive travellers includes reception of their luggage with liability for its safety. This responsibility is of a special character, sometimes known as strict liability, as it amounts in effect to insuring such property against loss or damage. Because the proprietor can become liable even when he or his staff are not negligent he has a higher duty of care than a private hotel proprietor.

The proprietor would be entitled to refuse property which is not luggage so long as he has adequate reason for doing so, such as something which might cause fire or other damage. He has no right to enquire whether any goods are the property of the guest, and a guest questioned about ownership could refuse to tell him. However, should the proprietor suspect that any goods had been stolen or might prove dangerous, he would be wise to notify the police.

Extent of Liability for Guests' Property

The general provisions which apply to the proprietor's responsibility for the property of guests are as follow:

1. He cannot avoid liability for loss or damage by proving that he was not negligent, and would be liable whether the loss or damage was caused by a thief from outside, or by a member of his staff, or by another guest. He cannot contract out of this liability by the exhibition of a notice disclaiming responsibility.

2. He can avoid liability if he can prove that the loss or damage was caused by negligence of the guest, by act of God (which in Scotland includes fire), or by act of the Queen's enemies.

3. He can limit his liability by the exhibition of the notice which forms the schedule to the Hotel Proprietors Act (see page 142) subject to certain conditions. The Act makes the following provisions as to the extent of the proprietor's liability:

(a) he is liable to make good damage as well as loss;

(b) at the time of the loss or damage, sleeping accommodation at the hotel must have been engaged for the traveller;

(c) the loss or damage must have occurred during the period commencing with the midnight immediately preceding, and ending with the midnight immediately following, for which the traveller was a guest at the hotel and entitled to use the accommodation so engaged. It should be noted that luggage sent in advance will not become subject to strict liability until the day the guest is due to arrive;

(d) liability does not extend to any vehicle, any property left in a vehicle, or to any horse or other live animal, its harness or other equipment;

(e) the maximum amount of liability to any one guest is limited to fifty pounds in respect of any one article, or one hundred pounds in the aggregate, except where—

  (i) the property was lost, stolen or damaged through the default, neglect or wilful act of the proprietor or some employee of his, or

  (ii) the property was deposited by or on behalf of the guest expressly for safe custody with the proprietor or some employee of his, authorised or appearing to be authorised, for the purpose, and if so requested by the proprietor or that employee, in a container fastened or sealed by the depositor, or

  (iii) at a time after the guest had arrived, either the property in question was offered for deposit and the proprietor or his employee had refused it, or the guest or someone acting on his behalf wished to offer it but, through the default of the proprietor or his employee, had been unable to do so.

The limitation of liability under (e) can only be achieved by the exhibition of the notice, which must be printed in plain type and conspicuously displayed in a place where it can be conveniently read by guests at or near the reception office or desk, or where there is no reception office or desk, at or near the main entrance to the hotel. In the absence of the notice, liability could be unlimited.

It should be noted that the foregoing provisions relate to the proprietor's obligations as imposed on him by the Act. He may also incur liability under a contract of bailment, as for example accepting a car in the hotel garage, but this kind of transaction could be made subject to conditions so long as the conditions are reasonable in the circumstances. Under the Unfair Contract Terms Act, the proprietor cannot escape the consequences of his own or an employee's negligence.

Negligence
Where an allegation of negligence arises in connection with loss of or damage to a guest's property, whether against the proprietor or a guest, the relevant facts will determine whether the proprietor escapes liability altogether, whether he retains limited liability or whether he loses the protection of the Act. Questions of this nature are best passed to the hotel's insurance company with the fullest details.

Deposit for Safe Custody
If a guest so requests, the proprietor is obliged to accept for safe custody any property brought to the hotel by the guest, other than a car or live animal. He may, if he thinks fit, require any items to be put in a container and fastened or sealed by the depositor. If this is not done he may decline the unlimited responsibility which deposit for safe custody involves. This provision obviates the necessity for small articles of value to be received in detail, such as money or jewellery; the proprietor can then give a receipt for a sealed package without any note of the contents. The guest on surrendering the receipt would be entitled to the return of the sealed package in the same condition as when it was handed in.

It is not necessary for the guest to deposit his property personally with the proprietor; some other person may act on behalf of the guest and the proprietor may authorise an employee to receive property from guests for this purpose. Unreasonable refusal to accept such property when offered would deprive the proprietor of the protection of the Act.

Proprietor's Lien
Subject to the provisions of the Act concerning cars and live animals, the proprietor has a lien on the goods of a guest for the

amount of his account, i.e. a right to retain them until his account has been paid. The lien applies only to goods received when the guest is received and continues only while the property remains at the hotel and while the guest remains a guest. The right of lien arises from the proprietor's obligation to receive all respectable travellers.

It is not material whether a traveller stays the night or not, and if he only takes a meal and has, for example, a suitcase with him, it could be detained by the proprietor if his account is not paid. If the suitcase was lost in such circumstances, the proprietor would not be responsible for it unless sleeping accommodation had been engaged.

The lien can be exercised on any goods which the guest brings with him, whether they are his own property or not, provided the proprietor is not aware that they belonged to someone else when received.

The proprietor has no right to detain the guest, or any clothes he may be wearing, if the account is not paid. To attempt to do so would amount to an assault.

In addition to his right of lien, the proprietor has a right of sale, subject to certain conditions:

    1. No sale may take place until the goods have been in the custody of the proprietor for six weeks without the account having been paid.

    2. At least one month before the sale, the proprietor must put an advertisement in one London newspaper and one other paper circulating in the district where the goods or some of them have been left, containing notice of the intended sale, with a description of the goods to be sold and the name of the owner or person depositing them where known.

    3. On demand, the proprietor must pay to the guest concerned the surplus, if any, arising from the sale of his goods, after allowing for the debt and the costs of the sale.

WHERE THE ACT DOES NOT APPLY

A. Residential Premises
These premises would include private hotels, guest houses, boarding houses and others where some service is provided for short or long-term residents. These differ from hotels in the following respects:

at an Hotel	*at a Private Hotel*
Respectable travellers have a right to be received provided accommodation is available.	No one has a right to accommodation; visitors may be accepted by agreement with the proprietor,
Loss of or damage to a guest's property is the responsibility of the proprietor unless the guest has been negligent.	The proprietor is not liable for a guest's property unless he, the proprietor, is proved to have been negligent.
The proprietor has a right to detain a guest's property as security for an unpaid account.	The proprietor has no right to detain a guest's property in such circumstances.

Choice of Guest
The private hotel proprietor reserves to himself the right to pick and choose his guests, and does not hold himself out as being willing to receive anyone who calls. He makes a separate contract, either written or verbal, and may in practice make all or most of his contracts in advance of the date when they are to take effect, e.g. for a holiday period.

As he is unwilling to accept the responsibilities of an hotel proprietor, he has to conduct his business in such a way that his legal position is clear. The use of the word 'private' would help, but if it is not used some other evidence may be needed if, for example, a guest claims for lost property under the impression that the business is within scope of the Act. Such evidence might be provided by records showing refusal of accommodation on grounds other than lack of a room, such as where very young children are concerned.

The exhibition of a card in a window, marked 'vacancies', might indicate a willingness to receive anyone who calls, but if this were exhibited only at irregular intervals it might not be regarded as normal practice. If no food is provided, or only breakfast, the business would be outside the scope of the Act.

Discrimination on grounds of race would be out of order in a private hotel as in any other kind of business, but whether or not an hotel catering for 'men only' or 'women only' would offend against the Sex Discrimination Act has not so far been tested.

Guests' Property

Although the private hotel proprietor does not have the strict liability of the hotel proprietor, he must nevertheless take due and proper care of guests' property so as to avoid any claim that he or his staff have been negligent.

Sometimes a notice is exhibited in bedrooms in terms such as the following:

> *The proprietor of this establishment will not be responsible for any articles belonging to visitors unless deposited at the office for safe custody.*

Such a notice may serve as a warning to guests to take care of their property, but it does not follow that the proprietor would necessarily be responsible for any loss which occurred even if articles were deposited for safe custody. To succeed in a claim, the guest must prove the proprietor or a member of his staff to have been negligent.

Unpaid Bills

As a private hotel proprietor has no right of lien on a guest's property for an unpaid account, he must not detain it. Should he attempt to do so, and the guest called a policeman, the proprietor would be obliged to release it. His only redress then would be to sue the guest in the appropriate court (the county court in England and Wales, the sheriff court in Scotland.)

B. Non-residential Premises

As a non-resident cannot claim against an hotel for loss of or damage to his property, it follows that a similar situation exists in restaurants, public houses and other non-residential premises. Such premises are, in effect, a type of shop, where the proprietor is under no legal obligation to serve anyone and has no responsibility for a customer's property.

The proprietor would, however, be responsible for any articles which may come into his possession as bailee as, for example, where a guest or customer leaves his hat and coat while taking a meal. So long as the hat and coat are accepted by the proprietor or an employee, he is entitled to their return in the same condition as when they were handed in on surrender of the receipt. The exhibition of a disclaimer notice purporting to exonerate the proprietor from liability will only be effective if brought to the attention of the depositor beforehand, and even then may be challenged under the Unfair Contract Terms Act 1977 (see page 133).

HOTEL BOOKINGS

Many of the points which follow are common to all kinds of residential establishment where accommodation is offered for reward and it makes no difference whether the Hotel Proprietors Act applies or not.

Advance Bookings

A guest wishing to book a room at an hotel or guest house at some future date may do so by personal call, by telephone or by correspondence. In order that a valid contract may exist between the proprietor and the guest, there must be:

1. A definite offer of accommodation by the proprietor, and
2. An unconditional acceptance of that offer within a reasonable time.

What may be regarded as a reasonable time would depend on the circumstances. It would probably be quite reasonable to take a week to consider an offer for a date three or four months ahead, whereas it might be unreasonable to take a week to consider an offer for a date a fortnight ahead, especially if the offer related to a high-season period.

While a verbal contract is quite legal, the parties might be uncertain as to its exact terms in the event of a difference arising. It is therefore preferable that all contracts to take effect at a future date should be in writing and that the terms should be clear and specific, in order to avoid the risk of misunderstanding. If there is a genuine doubt as to the intentions of the parties, it might be difficult to prove the existence of a valid contract, because to constitute a valid contract there must be agreement between the parties. A telephone booking should be made subject to confirmation by a given time, and a personal booking made by the guest or someone acting on his behalf should be regarded as provisional until confirmed in writing.

An offer of accommodation may be withdrawn before it has been accepted, but notice of such withdrawal is effective only when it reaches the other party. A mere enquiry for a room or a request to reserve a room cannot be regarded as a contract.

Where an offer of accommodation is made by letter, or is made verbally subject to confirmation by post, a contract comes into existence when the guest's letter of acceptance has been *posted*. If the accommodation has in the meantime been let to another party, the proprietor, if he has no alternative rooms available, may be called upon by the guest to find him equivalent accommodation elsewhere. Should the proprietor fail to do so, and the guest himself finds the alternative accommodation but at a higher cost, he can call on the proprietor with whom he made the first contract to compensate him for the trouble and expense to which he has been put; to succeed in such a claim, he would have to show that he had no option but to pay the higher terms. Liability of this nature can be avoided by making all offers of accommodation, especially at busy times of the year, subject to the room being available on *receipt* of reply.

Deposits

Where a deposit is paid at the time of reservation, this may be regarded as an earnest of good faith where there is nothing in writing to prove the contract or as a payment on account. In the event of subsequent cancellation by the guest, the return of the deposit would depend on the circumstances. Where adequate notice has been given so that re-letting is reasonably certain, the deposit might be returned immediately with or without a deduction to cover any expense of re-letting. If only short notice is given, and there is little or no prospect of re-letting, the proprietor may wish to claim compensation for breach of contract; in that event, the deposit should be retained and set off against the claim. The guest cannot demand the return of the deposit in full and, if it is a small one, there is no obligation to return it.

Whether, in practice, it is prudent to return a deposit must be for the proprietor to decide.

Booking on behalf of a Party

Where one person seeks to book accommodation on behalf of a party the proprietor needs a clear understanding as to the name or names of the guest or guests who will be responsible for the payment of his account; if more than one person is involved addresses of all should be obtained.

Booking by an Agent

Consideration must also be given to the proprietor's position in accepting a booking from a travel agent. Normally an agent can make a contract on behalf of a guest without becoming personally liable for the fulfilment of the contract, and may not disclose the home address of the guest. Many agents will be parties to a code of booking practice designed to ensure that no problems will arise, but should this not be the case the proprietor must realise that, should the guest fail to arrive, any claim would have to be made against the agent, who in the normal course should have been paid by the guest.

Cancelled Bookings

Cancellation by either party of a valid contract for the reservation of accommodation entitles the other party to claim compensation for any loss directly incurred thereby, unless the cancellation is by mutual consent. This subject falls into two parts—cancellation by an hotel, and cancellation by a guest.

Where an hotel, having reserved a room for a guest, fails to let him have the use of it at the agreed time for any reason, the guest could claim for any loss incurred as a direct result of the failure of the hotel to complete its part of the contract. Such circumstances might arise where an hotel has made a duplicate booking in error, where the hotel has changed hands between the making of the contract and the date for its performance and the new proprietor has been unaware of the arrangements made by his predecessor, or where the illness of a guest has made it impossible for the next guest to occupy the room on the agreed date. In any of such circumstances, the hotel has an obligation to find equivalent accommodation for the guest elsewhere and, failing this, to offer some compensation.

Where a guest arrives after the due date but within the period booked, the legal position would depend upon the exact terms of the contract. A guest might, for example, reserve a room from one Saturday to the next and actually arrive on the intervening Tuesday expecting to find the room at his disposal. If the hotel, not having heard from the guest on the first Saturday, had assumed he was not coming and had re-let the room, it could be liable to compensate him for extra expense he might incur in finding other accommodation. Difficulties of this kind might be avoided by having a clear understanding in the contract that the guest will arrive on a certain date, or trying to communicate with him after non-arrival, or by making any re-letting conditional on the original guest not coming.

Where the contract is broken by the guest, either by specific cancellation or by failure to arrive at the due time, the proprietor would be entitled to claim compensation for his actual loss and no more. He may not claim what amounts to a penalty or a fine. He must endeavour to minimise his loss by re-letting, and if a complete re-letting is achieved on the same terms, the original guest is relieved of liability; if there is a partial re-letting, the claim must be correspondingly reduced.

No claim may be made on a defaulting guest until after the date when the booking would have expired, as only then can the actual loss be computed. If long notice of cancellation has been given, allowing adequate time for re-letting, it is doubtful whether a claim by the hotel would succeed even if it had incurred a loss.

Mention must be made of circumstances which might justify the repudiation of a contract by a guest on the ground of misrepresentation by the hotel, or for the reason that the appointments, service, food, etc., were not of a standard consistent with the terms charged. Furthermore, the guest now has statutory remedies under the Trade Descriptions Act and under the Misrepresentation Act 1967 which, in appropriate circumstances, could enable him to avoid liability under the contract and to claim damages for any loss sustained as a direct consequence.

Terms and Conditions
The Tourism (Sleeping Accommodation Price Display) Order 1977 requires current prices to be displayed in the reception area or at the entrance of hotels and guest houses having four or more letting bedrooms or accommodation for eight or more persons. The prices must show the cost of a single room and a double room for adults, and whether they include VAT, service charge, or any meals and, if so, the respective amounts. Where charges are not standard throughout, maximum and minimum figures must be stated. Charges applicable to rooms normally let for 21 days or more may be ignored. The local weights and measures authority is responsible for enforcement, and there is a maximum penalty of £200 for failure to comply without reasonable excuse.

Where quotations are given by post or in a brochure, or over the telephone, it is important that full details are made known if they are intended to form part of a contract because once accepted they cannot be varied, except by mutual consent.

A booking for an indefinite period would, in the absence of specific agreement, be subject to a week's notice.

GUESTS IN RESIDENCE

Registration

Every person staying at an hotel, guest house or boarding house for one night or more, whatever his nationality, must, if 16 years of age or over, have his full name, nationality and date of arrival entered in the register. It is the duty of the proprietor to keep a register of guests and to see that the required information is entered therein (see Appendix II).

It is not now a requirement of the law that guests must themselves enter this information in the register, though it is normal practice for them to do so; they may give it to the proprietor for him to enter. The register may be a book or on cards or loose leaves.

British subjects are not required to give their address, and they do not commit an offence by registering in a false name. Guests not of British nationality must add particulars of their passport or other certificate of identity and, when departing, the date of leaving and place to which they are proceeding with their address if known.

Particulars of each guest must be shown separately, and it is not sufficient for husband and wife to sign as 'Mr. and Mrs.' Guests sleeping out should give the necessary information to the proprietor with whom they booked.

The register must be kept available for inspection by the police if required, and must be retained for 12 months after completion.

Divorce evidence

An hotel may sometimes be required to supply evidence in divorce cases, by providing witnesses who can testify to the presence in the hotel of certain persons at a particular time. This evidence cannot be refused if demanded by a court; the court may wish to inspect the register, and members of the staff may be called by one side or the other to give evidence. Persons actually attending court can claim for their expenses and any loss of wages they may have suffered, but the hotel itself cannot claim for any loss it has incurred.

Requests for information in advance of proceedings can be refused, but it is best to pass them to the hotel's solicitors.

Access to hotel
Where it is the practice to close the hotel at night, provision must be made so that guests wishing to be out late are not locked out, e.g. by the offer of a key. Any improper restraint might constitute a personal trespass.

Difficult guests
A guest who behaves improperly, annoys other guests, or makes himself a nuisance, may be required to leave an hotel, whether he happens to be a traveller or not. If there is conduct likely to cause a breach of the peace and the guest will not leave willingly, a reasonable amount of force may be used to put him out. If necessary, the police should be informed.

Guest of unsound mind
A guest who is not of sound mind cannot enter into a valid contract. If insanity develops after making the contract, the hotel would be entitled to terminate it on giving the usual notice, or if the guest is obviously or dangerously insane the contract could be terminated at once.

Infectious illness
Where a guest contracts an infectious disease while staying at an hotel, the local Medical Officer of Health must be notified and his directions followed. A doctor attending the guest will know which diseases are notifiable, and if it is one which necessitates fumigation of the room and its contents before it can be re-let; it would be an offence to allow another person to

use it until it had been fumigated. Any loss incurred by the hotel as a direct result of such an illness would be chargeable to the guest concerned, but can be covered by insurance.

Where there is a case of infectious illness in an hotel, the proprietor is under an obligation to warn other guests so that they may take any necessary precautions; this is particularly important where children are concerned.

Death at an hotel

If a guest dies at an hotel and there are no known relatives or friends, a doctor or the local medical officer will be able to advise about disposal of the body. If the death is sudden or unnatural, e.g. a suicide, the coroner has to be informed, preferably by a doctor.

Finding of property

Where property is found on hotel or restaurant premises and the owner is unknown, the question will arise as to its disposal. The law is not clear on this subject, but it appears that the finder has a good title except against:

1. the true owner, and
2. the person on whose premises the property is found.

If the finder is an employee of the occupier, he must be regarded as finding for his employer. Before any title can be acquired by a person other than the rightful owner, there must be some proof that the owner had abandoned it, otherwise the finder must hold it at the disposal of the rightful owner in case he should claim it. How long would be a reasonable time for the finder so to hold it would depend on circumstances and especially on the value of the property.

Finding can become the criminal offence of theft when the finder believes the owner can be discovered by taking steps, and the lost article had not been intentionally abandoned by its owner, yet forthwith resolves to appropriate it.

Where property of any value is found, it is better to hand it to the police with an account of the circumstances of finding.

In Scotland, any property found which can be regarded as lost property should be handed to the police within 48 hours. If not claimed within six months, the finder could receive it back from the police as his own property. There is a duty on the finder to communicate with the owner first if his whereabouts can be ascertained.

Registered letters for guests
The following account of a case which was taken to court by a guest shows the responsibility of hotels for registered packages addressed to guests. In this case, a guest was sent a wrist watch by registered post, and the package was signed for by a porter. On behalf of the Post Office it was said that an employee's signature was acceptable as a receipt. The porter had no authority from his employer to receive packages or to sign for them. The proprietor denied having received the package, but the court decided that the porter was a sufficiently responsible person to whom the postman was justified in handing letters. There was no evidence that the proprietor had ever made a request to the Post Office as to the signatures they might accept. In the circumstances, the proprietor was held responsible.

Damage to property by guests
There are many ways in which damage to hotel property may be caused by guests. Carpets, furniture and linen may be damaged by cigarette burns, heavy articles may be dropped in washbasins, stains may be caused by ink, cosmetics or chemicals, towels may be cut by razors, mirrors may be cracked, and so on. If damage can be proved to have been caused by negligence of a guest, he can be made to pay, but it is not usually easy to obtain sufficient evidence to enable an hotel to recover anything from a guest. Where damage is caused by accident, no claim would be successful. While risks of this kind can be covered by insurance, the hotel would be expected to bear minor losses.

Guests who have left
Where a guest, having paid his account, leaves some of his property on the premises and it is not removed within a reasonable time, the proprietor may inform him that unless the property is removed by a certain date it will be sold to defray expenses.

Should this course fail or efforts to trace him are unsuccessful, the proprietor could safely dispose of it.

Where a letter arrives at an hotel for a guest after his departure, the proprietor is responsible for its safety. If the guest's address is known, the letter should be re-directed; if not, it should be marked 'gone away' and returned to the Post Office. Retention of a guest's letter could be a criminal offence.

GUESTS AND CUSTOMERS—GENERALLY

Safety
Under the Occupiers Liability Act 1957, the occupier of premises has a duty of care towards his lawful visitors which is referred to as the 'common duty of care' and means a duty to take such care as in all the circumstances of the case is reasonable to see that the visitor will be reasonably safe in using the premises for the purpose for which he is invited or permitted by the occupier to be there. The occupier must be prepared for children to be less careful than adults, and he is entitled to expect that a person in the exercise of his calling (e.g. an electrician) will appreciate and guard against any special risks ordinarily incidental to it.

These provisions apply to guests and customers, postmen, tradespeople, builders and decorators, window cleaners and others, and the occupier should cover such risks to which they may be exposed by insurance.

The occupier's duty of care does not extend to parts of the premises not intended to be used by guests, such as staff quarters, and such parts should be clearly identified, with suitable lighting at night.

Fire Precautions
Most premises in the hotel and catering industry are now covered by legislation requiring the proprietor to have a fire certificate. The Fire Precautions Act 1971 provides that the owner, occupier or person in charge of premises used for the provision of sleeping accommodation or entertainment or for other purposes involving access by the public, must apply for such a certificate.

GUESTS AND CUSTOMERS—GENERALLY

A fire certificate allows premises to be used for a specified purpose (e.g. an hotel), subject to the provision of means of escape in case of fire, and fire-fighting appliances reasonably required.

There is a right of appeal to a magistrates' court (the sheriff in Scotland) against refusal to issue a fire certificate or as to its contents. Penalties can be imposed for failure to observe the requirements of a certificate.

Some local authorities make loans to assist proprietors of small businesses to meet the cost of fire precautions requirements if they cannot obtain adequate finance elsewhere.

Race Relations

Legislation designed to promote racial harmony applies to almost every business in the hotel and catering industry, and the Commission for Racial Equality has powers to curb discrimination with recourse to the courts if necessary. There would be evidence of discrimination when a person refuses or neglects to afford a member of the public access to a public place or any services or facilities available there in the like manner and on the like terms as are available to other members of the public resorting thereto.

Small establishments are exempted where the proprietor lives on the premises, shares some of the facilities (e.g. a bathroom) with guests, and there is accommodation for not more than six persons.

Trade Descriptions

The Trade Descriptions Act 1968 is enforceable by the local weights and measures authority. It prohibits the use in connection with a sale of goods of a false trade description, written or oral, which is false to a material degree and includes one which while not false is misleading.

In connection with the provision of services, the Act makes it an offence for any person in the course of a trade or business to make a statement which he knows to be false, or recklessly to make a statement which is false as to any of the following matters:

(a) The provision in the course of any trade or business of any services, accommodation or facilities provided.

(b) The nature of any services, accommodation or facilities provided in the course of any trade or business.

(c) The time at which, manner in which or persons by whom any services, accommodation or facilities are so provided.

(d) The examination, approval or evaluation by any person of any services, accommodation or facilities so provided.

(e) The location or amenities of any accommodation so provided.

The Act applies to statements in advertisements, brochures and menus, and also to information given either in writing or orally about goods or services available.

Penalties for offences are: on summary conviction, a fine not exceeding £400; on conviction on indictment, a fine (no maximum specified) or imprisonment not exceeding two years, or both.

In any proceedings under this Act it would be a defence for the person charged to prove that the commission of the offence was due to a mistake or to reliance on information supplied to him, or to the act or default of any person, an accident or some other cause beyond his control. To support such a defence, he must prove that he took all reasonable precautions and exercised all due diligence to avoid the commission of the offence by himself or any person under his control.

Payment of Accounts

The proprietors of hotel and catering businesses are entitled to expect payment of their accounts in cash, and may refuse cheques, which are not legal tender. Bank notes are legal tender to any amount, coins up to and including 10p are legal tender up to £5 and 50p coins up to £10.

Where a guest wishes to pay by cheque, it is desirable that he should hand it to the management in sufficient time for it to be cleared before he leaves. The granting of credit facilities is a matter for the management who may, for example, be willing to accept credit cards issued by a bank or travel organisation.

Unpaid Bills

As explained earlier, an hotel proprietor may detain a guest's property as security for an unpaid bill. A guest house proprietor may not do this. If a guest obtains credit by what appears to be fraud, the police may be summoned though they will be interested only in the crime itself and not in securing redress for the proprietor; as an alternative, the guest could be asked to leave an article of value as evidence of good faith. This advice would also apply to a customer at a restaurant or public house who could not pay; liquor must be paid for in cash.

Where a defaulting guest's or customer's name and address are known, he may be sued in the county court (the sheriff court in Scotland). A person who makes a practice of obtaining food and/or accommodation knowing he has not the means to pay can be convicted for obtaining property or pecuniary advantage by deception under the Theft Act.

STAFF

ENGAGEMENT, EMPLOYMENT AND DISMISSAL

Where two parties enter into an agreement whereby one works for and under the control of the other, a contract of employment exists. Such a contract may be made orally or its terms and conditions expressed in writing; there are a number of statutory requirements. If the contract does not cover every eventuality which may arise between the parties some doubt about their rights and obligations may exist which would have to be settled according to their intentions at the time the contract was made or, if these intentions are unknown or indefinite, according to the customs of the trade or the law governing the matter.

The legal relationship between employer and employee is based on Common Law, consisting of cases decided by the courts mainly concerned with domestic service, formerly known as the Law of Master and Servant. While principles generally remain unchanged, details have been substantially amended by legislation, some of which is intended to harmonise the law throughout the countries of the European Economic Community.

Legislation tends to be all-embracing, seldom allowing for differences between manufacturing and service industries, with the result that the ultimate effect of new statutes on the hotel and catering industry is not altogether clear and straightforward. Some consolidation with existing legislation, and the incorporation of new provisions, may be expected to follow, but meanwhile this chapter shows the position in mid-1978.

Two changes affecting small businesses have extended the scope of earlier legislation. Hitherto, the rights of employees in such matters as redundancy did not apply where the number of staff was less than four, and also where near relatives of the employer were concerned. Now, all employees have similar rights, with the sole exception of husband/wife employment. There is thus no longer any significance in regarding certain employees as domestic servants.

Before referring to different aspects of the law, it will be helpful to set out the basic principles as they apply to both parties:

Obligations of the Employer
In the absence of agreement to the contrary, the employer is regarded as undertaking:

1. to provide work as arranged;
2. to pay wages when due;
3. to take all reasonable precautions for his employee's safety during the performance of his duties—see Health and Safety at Work Act (page 46);
4. to idemnify his employee against liability for loss or injury while acting within the scope of his authority in obeying his employer's instructions. An employee cannot claim against his employer for loss or injury attributable to his (the employee's) own fault. Where an employee commits a wrongful act, he will be liable to the third party; if the wrongful act arises out of the employment and within its scope, both employee and employer could be liable.

An employer is obliged to insure against bodily injury sustained by his employees arising out of their employment, which must include injury when using machinery provided by the employer which has a defect, even though the defect can be traced to an error on the part of the manufacturer.

Duties of the Employee
The following duties are inherent in a contract of employment, unless there is agreement to the contrary:

1. to give personal service; he cannot send a deputy except by special arrangement;
2. to obey orders which the employer or someone acting on his behalf is justified in giving under the contract; he is entitled to refuse an order which might involve risk of injury, e.g. external window-cleaning without safety support;

3. to use reasonable care and skill appropriate to the performance of the duties for which he is employed;

4. to act honestly and in good faith towards his employer;

5. to account for money and property received on behalf of his employer;

6. to refrain from disclosing to a third party information of a confidential nature received by him in the course of his employment.

Labour Relations

Personnel management is an art all employers have to master, and where there are also guests and customers on the premises, there should be ample opportunity to acquire skill in creating goodwill. For this reason, relations with staff depend increasingly on common sense rather than law. But occasionally some problem may arise which may not be simple to solve. In this industry, the best source of advice is likely to be a trade association.

A new organisation, known as the Advisory, Conciliation and Arbitration Service (ACAS) has been set up under the Trade Union and Labour Relations Act, which is independent of Government though staffed by the Department of Employment. It has responsibility for giving advice to employers and employees either individually or through an employers' association or trade union. Its purpose is to endeavour to settle disputes by conciliation on request or on its own initiative. Where appropriate, and by agreement of the parties, it can refer disputes to the Central Arbitration Committee, which can make enforceable decisions.

The Council of ACAS consists of a full-time chairman, two other independent members and three representatives each of employers and employees. Its headquarters are in London, but it can meet in other parts of the country, including Scotland, as necessary.

Trade Unions

An employee has a basic right to join, or not to join, a trade union of his choice, and his decision must not result in any penalty or discrimination on the part of his employer. An employee dismissed solely because he joined a union would have a valid claim to compensation on appeal to an industrial tribunal.

Trade unions have had representation on wages councils for more than thirty years, and any approach to an employer would have as its objective better conditions than are provided in wages orders. An employer cannot be compelled to recognise a union for collective bargaining purposes; the union could, however, refer a recognition issue to ACAS which then has an obligation to ascertain the views of the employees concerned. But ACAS can only make a recommendation, as it has no power to enforce any decision.

Where an employer decides to recognise a trade union, certain obligations follow, namely, to co-operate with the union by providing information about his business sufficient to enable realistic collective bargaining to take place, but not items likely to injure the business; to allow union officials to have time off to attend to trade union duties which affect the employees concerned; to consult with the union where dismissal or redundancy affects the union's members.

ACAS may issue codes of practice to serve as a guide, without legal commitment, in determining what is reasonable when dealing with the foregoing matters.

Engagement

While an employer is generally free to engage any staff he chooses, he needs to exercise discretion when advertising vacancies and in making a choice between applicants, to avoid a claim of unfair discrimination on grounds of sex or race. All jobs must be seen to be open to anyone with the requisite qualifications who cares to apply, and where there is a different job title for men and women, e.g. waiter and waitress, both should be eligible.

Some exceptions are recognised. The Sex Discrimination Act allows discrimination in the following circumstances:

1. where being a man or a woman could be regarded as a genuine occupational qualification as, for example, in entertainment, to ensure authenticity;

2. to preserve privacy or decency;

3. where accommodation or facilities on an employer's premises cannot reasonably be made suitable for both;

4. where employment is intended for a married couple.

Exceptions on racial grounds would include employing, for example, Chinese staff in a Chinese restaurant, where nationality could be regarded as a genuine occupational qualification. Other exceptions may arise as the result of industrial tribunal decisions.

It is for the person who seeks redress for alleged unfair discrimination to make a claim to a tribunal, when the prospective employer would be given an opportunity to show that his choice was made on other grounds and that he had acted reasonably in the circumstances.

When deciding how long the employment is intended to continue the employer may have a choice. There are four customary arrangements in this industry, which are listed with the statutory obligations and rights attaching in each instance:

indefinite: *employer* to provide written statement (see below) within 13 weeks, where weekly hours are 16 or more; *employee* will have right after 26 weeks' service not to be unfairly dismissed; a right to maternity leave after 2 years; a right to redundancy pay after 2 years;

temporary: less than 26 weeks, e.g. seasonal—*employer* to provide written statement within 13 weeks, where weekly hours are 16 or more, which should include terminal date;

part-time: weekly hours 8 to 15—after five years' service, *employer* to provide written statement; after five years' service, *employee* has right not to be unfairly dismissed, and a right to redundancy pay;

occasional: e.g. for functions; both sides free to agree terms and conditions.

Written Statement

The statement referred to above must contain the following information:

1. the names of the employer and employee;

2. the date the employment commenced; where any employment by a previous employer counts as part of the employee's continuous service (e.g. where the purchaser of a business takes over the vendor's staff) the date on which that employment began;

3. the job title—where possible this should correspond with the relevant title in a wages order;

4. the scale or rate of remuneration or the method of calculating remuneration;

5. the intervals at which remuneration is payable;

6. any terms and conditions relating to hours of work;

7. entitlement to holidays, including public holidays and holiday pay;

8. any terms and conditions relating to incapacity for work due to sickness or injury, including any provision for sick pay, pension and pension schemes;

9. the length of notice to determine the contract, by the employer and by the employee;

10. the procedure for remedying any grievance, to include any disciplinary rules, and the name of the person to whom the employee can refer if dissatisfied with the decision of an immediate superior.

These particulars should be those applying at a date not earlier than one week before the statement is given and may, if appropriate, refer the employee to some document, such as a wages order, which he has reasonable opportunity to read during employment. Changes in any of these particulars must be notified to the employee within one month, either by means of a notice which he can read during employment or by an individual notice for him to keep.

Health and Safety
What have hitherto been an employer's Common Law duties concerning the health and safety of his employees while at work are now statutory obligations, with general supervision by the Health and Safety Commission and Executive. Employers are now required, so far as reasonably practicable, to ensure the health and safety of their employees while at work, with par-

ticular regard to safe premises, working environment and work systems, maintenance of machines and equipment, handling of materials, with adequate precautions against risks. They are required to ensure that their employees are fully informed and instructed with due regard for their welfare. Employees, too, have an obligation to take care of their own health and safety, with due consideration for others and co-operation with their employer.

Where five or more persons are employed on any premises, their employer must prepare and keep up-to-date a written safety policy, naming a person as having responsibility for safety, and listing risks and precautions to prevent accidents. The Department of Employment has issued a leaflet of general guidance in preparing a safety policy, but so far no code of practice with particular reference to this industry is available. Meantime, provisions of the Offices, Shops and Railway Premises Act and of the Food Hygiene Regulations concerned with health and safety remain in operation.

Inspectors will have power to enter premises concerned at any reasonable time and to serve an Improvement Notice on an employer where working conditions involve unacceptable risks to health and safety, requiring specified changes to be made; they have additional power to close premises where risks are deemed to be excessive. An employer could appeal to an industrial tribunal against an unreasonable demand.

Absence from Duty
Item 8 of the written statement should make clear what payment, if any, an employee is entitled to receive when absent through illness, in addition to National Insurance Sickness Benefit. If this is not done, and he is a weekly-paid employee, normal wages might be due. Where appropriate, words could be added to require a medical certificate to be provided within a specified time; this would serve as an assurance that the employee regarded the contract as still in existence.

Where an employee is absent without informing his employer within a reasonable time, he might be regarded as having left without notice. This situation may arise where an employee is dissatisfied and finds another job. Although the employer has a right of redress it is seldom practicable to take any action. If accrued holiday remuneration is due under a wages order this is, strictly speaking, payable on termination of the contract and cannot legally be held as damages for breach of contract; the employee or an inspector of the Department of Employment could sue him for it. Some wages orders, however, provide for the withholding of part of accrued holiday remuneration where notice is not given.

There are certain circumstances in which an employer is obliged to allow time off or leave of absence:

1. An employee with public duties to perform is entitled to reasonable time off without pay. These duties would include acting as a justice of the peace, member of a local authority, statutory tribunal, regional or area health authority (a health board in Scotland), the governing body of certain educational establishments, or a water authority (a river purification board in Scotland).

2. A woman with more than two years' service with her employer is entitled to maternity leave if she is able and willing to continue working until 11 weeks before the birth of her child is expected and wishes to return after the birth. She alone has the decision whether to leave and if her employer dismisses her solely on account of her pregnancy she would have a valid claim for compensation. Should she not be able to continue until the 11th week, her employer is obliged to find her an alternative job if available.

She must give three weeks' notice of her intention to stop work, in writing if her employer so requests. She then becomes entitled to maternity leave, with payment for the first six weeks of absence at 90% of normal wages (maximum £80, less flat-rate National Insurance Maternity Benefit), which her employer can recover from the Maternity Pay Fund. Provided she gives three weeks' notice of her intention to return after the birth, her job must be kept open for her or a suitable alternative provided when the time comes.

Within 29 weeks after the birth she has to give one week's notice of the date of her intended return, which her employer can postpone for up to four weeks. She can maintain her right to return for a further four weeks on production of an appropriate medical certificate. Should her employer refuse reinstatement, or if in the meantime her job has become redundant, she may appeal to an industrial tribunal for compensation.

Payment of Wages
Wages are due for payment at the time agreed, which will normally be at the end of a pay period, weekly, fortnightly or monthly, as the case may be. It is not essential that payment should be made within the period for which it is due and a practice has developed in some other industries where payment is made some days after the end of a pay period; this is quite legal so long as it is part of the contract. The interval is known as 'lying time' and represents a period during which the employer can calculate the amount due from time sheets and other records.

Most employees in this industry will be within scope of a wages order, which may provide for a guaranteed minimum weekly payment subject to availability for work.

Payment for a broken period would depend on whether the employer was responsible for the break, e.g. by giving notice to expire otherwise than at the end of a pay period, when he would be liable; if the employee caused the break by leaving without proper notice, he would not normally be entitled to payment for the odd days.

Allowable deductions from wages include national insurance, income tax, pension contributions, and items specified in a wages order, such as the provision by the employer of board and lodging.

An employer may be required by a court to make a deduction from an employee's wages where it has made a maintenance order, when the amount deducted will be payable as the court directs.

During the nineteenth century, legislation known as the Truck Acts had to be introduced to ensure that employees received their wages in cash and not partly in kind as was the practice in some industries at the time. Although those Acts are still on the

Statute Book most of their provisions have become irrelevant. They might be applicable, however, where an employer sought to make deductions for breakages of glass and crockery, shortages of cash or damage to clothing provided by the employer. Deductions for any of these reasons can only be made if the employee's contract so provides and then only if the amount deducted is agreed at the time and represents no more than is necessary to compensate the employer for loss or damage due to the employee's admitted negligence.

By agreement with an employee, wages may be paid by cheque or direct into his bank account. During absence owing to illness payment normally due in cash may be made by postal order.

All employees are now entitled to an itemised pay statement on each occasion, setting out the gross amount due and the net amount after deductions, and where deductions are liable to vary, the relevant details; fixed deductions must be shown aggregated at least once a year.

Disciplinary Procedures
A code of practice, to give practical guidance without imposing legal obligations, has been prepared by ACAS to help employers devise disciplinary rules and procedures and operate them effectively. Their observance or non-observance could have some effect on tribunal decisions in unfair dismissal cases. The main recommendations are:

1. An employee should be given a copy of any rules which apply to him.

2. Any complaint against an employee should be brought to his notice and he should be given an opportunity to state his case, in company with a trade union representative or fellow employee of his choice, if he wishes.

3. Disciplinary action should not be taken until the complaint has been thoroughly investigated.

4. An immediate superior should not normally have power to dismiss without reference to senior management.

5. Except for gross misconduct, dismissal should not follow a first breach of discipline; an oral warning should be given for a minor offence, but for a more serious offence the

warning should be in writing, stating the nature of the offence and the consequences of a repetition.

6. Where the employee is a trade union official, no action beyond an oral warning should be taken until a more senior official has been consulted.

7. A criminal offence outside the scope of the employment is not an automatic ground for dismissal.

This code appears to have been designed for factory workers and while some provisions might be applicable to the hotel and catering industry there are several other matters which would need to be included to ensure reasonably complete coverage.

Termination of Contract

Statutory minimum periods of notice apply where normal hours of work are 16 or more per week, on the following scale:

after 4 weeks' employment   one week
after 2 years' employment   one week for every year to a maximum of 12 weeks

Where the normal hours of work are from 8 to 15 per week, an employee with five years' service qualifies for the week per year basis.

An employee must give one week's notice as a minimum.

In other cases, the period may be agreed, but in the absence of agreement should be reasonable in the circumstances.

During the first four weeks of employment an agreement could provide for very short notice in what may be regarded as a probationary period, so that dismissal for unsuitability, for example, could be at an hour's or even a minute's notice.

Should an employer dismiss an employee entitled to notice but wish him to leave at once, appropriate payment would be wages to the end of the notice period with, in addition, other emoluments he would have received if allowed to remain, which might include board and/or lodging, gratuities, or a share in a service charge.

Summary Dismissal

In certain circumstances, an employee could be dismissed without notice or wages in lieu, as for example:

1. for incompetence, not having the skill and ability he professed to have at the time of engagement, applicable to the type of work for which he was engaged;

2. for negligence—either one or more instances of a serious nature, or continued negligence likely to damage his employer's business—or habitual inattention to work;

3. for conduct calculated seriously to injure his employer's business, e.g. dissuading his customers from dealing with him, or disclosing to others confidential information received in the course of his employment;

4. for wilful disobedience to lawful and reasonable orders given by his employer or someone acting on his behalf;

5. for serious misconduct, inconsistent with the express or implied conditions of employment, e.g. dishonesty, habitual drunkenness, insolence. One isolated act might be sufficient if it was such as to prejudice the safe and proper conduct of the employer's business;

6. for accepting bribes and secret commissions.

Considerable care needs to be taken in dismissing an employee without notice in any of these circumstances, but a decision needs to be taken promptly, otherwise it could be argued that the employer had condoned the misconduct. There is added emphasis on the need for care now that an employee can claim compensation for unfair dismissal.

Where an employee is suspected of theft, the employer should not take it upon himself to give the employee into custody or to search his room or baggage; he should apply to a magistrate for a search warrant or report the matter to the police. It could be made a condition of employment that the employer had a right of search, and an employee would be breaking his contract if he refused to permit a search. Any person making a search in such circumstances must not use force nor take any action which in law might constitute an assault or unlawful detention.

An employee who has been dismissed in a proper manner, but who refuses to leave, may be forcibly removed provided no more force is used than is absolutely necessary. If such circumstances appear likely to cause a breach of the peace, it would be prudent to ask a policeman to be present if practicable; although he cannot take part in ejecting the employee, he must stop a breach of the peace occurring, and his presence is likely to make the use of force unnecessary.

Redundancy
An employer who dismisses an employee with not less than two years' continuous service, solely because he is redundant, may be liable to compensate him for loss of employment. For this purpose, redundancy means the ending of a particular job, such as an hotel discontinuing a night-porter service, or a restaurant changing to self-service; it could also apply where an employee is dismissed but not replaced. The amount of compensation is calculated according to age and length of service up to a maximum of 20 years. The employer will be able to recover some part of such payment (at present 41%) from the Redundancy Payments Fund, which is financed from National Insurance contributions.

The following scale applies:
    half a week's pay for each year of employment when the employee was aged 18 to 21;
    1 week's pay for each year of employment when the employee was aged 22 to 40;
    1½ weeks' pay for each year of employment when the employee was aged 41 to 64 (59 for a woman).

As an alternative, the employer may make a written offer of employment in another capacity within four weeks of the terminal date, and must allow the employee up to four weeks' experience in the new job before he decides whether to accept it.

An employee made redundant is entitled to reasonable paid time off to look for other employment.

Where an employer intends to make 10 or more employees redundant within 30 days, or 100 or more within 90 days, he must notify the Department of Employment at least 60 or 90 days respectively before the first dismissal is due to take effect.

Should any member of a recognised trade union be included in any redundancy proposal, the employer has an obligation to enter into negotiation with the union well before the first dismissal is due; notification alone is not sufficient.

Wrongful Dismissal

This term implies dismissal in breach of contract, e.g. without notice where there is entitlement to notice. Claims are at present heard by the courts, but may later come within the jurisdiction of tribunals. Damages, if awarded, would include wages for the period which ought to have been given, any emoluments which the employee was prevented from receiving, such as board and/or lodging, gratuities or share of a service charge, and some allowance for any additional period during which he is unemployed. To qualify for damages under this last heading, the employee must take all reasonable steps to obtain other employment.

Other Provisions about Dismissal

A dismissed employee with at least 26 weeks' service may request within 14 days a written statement of the reason for his dismissal; failure to supply the statement could involve the employer in payment of two weeks' wages as compensation.

An employee does not lose his right to compensation for unfair dismissal if he leaves of his own accord, provided he can prove that the reason for leaving was his employer's attitude towards him or prejudice against him. Such a case would be regarded as one of 'constructive dismissal'.

Industrial Tribunals

These are judicial bodies, with a legally-qualified chairman appointed by the Lord Chancellor (the Lord President in Scotland) and two other members appointed by the Secretary of State. They sit in various parts of the country as necessary, and their present functions are to hear cases arising out of redundancy, unfair dismissal and the Contracts of Employment Act, such as failure of an employer to provide a written statement when required.

An employer involved as respondent in a case has the right to contest it after receiving copy of an employee's or former employee's claim. If the claim is in respect of unfair dismissal a copy will also be sent to the conciliation officer of ACAS who will endeavour to resolve it without a tribunal hearing.

Proceedings before a tribunal are less formal than before a court, and as the ascertainment of the relevant facts is the primary function, the employer himself or one of his staff will normally be in the best position to present his case.

Where a tribunal decides an unfair dismissal case in favour of the employee, he will be asked whether he wishes to be (i) re-instated, which means treated as if he had not been dismissed, with all losses made up to him, or (ii) re-engaged in another capacity. His reply and any observations by the employer will have a bearing on the amount of compensation awarded. The redundancy payment scale will usually form the basis, with allowance being made for other factors, e.g. whether the employee contributed to his own dismissal.

Automatic Termination of Contract

A contract of employment is automatically terminated:

1. on the death of either party; if a breach of contract occurred before death, the deceased person's personal representative has right of action;

2. on the permanent incapacity of the employee, which is a question of fact in each case;

3. where the contract has become impossible to perform, e.g. destruction of premises by fire.

A contract is not terminated by the employer's insolvency, and there is provision in the Bankruptcy Act for preferential payment of wages. Where an employer is unable to make a redundancy payment or pay compensation awarded by a tribunal, the Department of Employment can take over the employer's obligations.

The bankruptcy of an employee has no effect on the contract unless bankruptcy is a disability in the circumstances.

The sale of the business does not relieve the employer of his responsibilities under the contract and it will be a matter for agreement with the purchaser whether he takes over the vendor's staff. If he does not do so, the vendor employer could be liable for redundancy payments and accrued holiday remuneration.

References

An employer is under no obligation to give a former employee a reference, but if one is given he must be careful not to say anything which is defamatory as, in certain circumstances, this might amount to libel (or slander, if spoken). Where a reference is given in good faith and believed to be true, and is given on an occasion of qualified privilege, no action can be maintained in respect of it unless it is given maliciously. A communication is privileged when it is given in discharge of a duty by one person to another who has an interest in receiving it, or where there is a common interest or reciprocal duty.

The law was clearly stated in a case where a barmaid sued her former employers for libel, alleging that a letter written by them had injured her reputation. The letter was sent as a reference to the tenant of another hotel who was considering employing her, and included the following words: 'We should tell you that Mrs. B left our employ mainly because of stock shortages. We must admit that we have experienced the same trouble since her departure, and if you decided to engage her you will no doubt be able to ensure that the stock in her charge is under control.'

In evidence on behalf of the defendant company, it was stated that Mrs. B had been employed by them for 11 years, first as waitress then as bar assistant. The company could not accuse her of any specific act of dishonesty but were dissatisfied with the stock-taking reports while she was in charge. The letter was intended to put the facts before a prospective employer and leave him to form his own opinion whether the loss of stock was due to her dishonesty or carelessness.

Giving judgment, the judge said it was most important to maintain the practice of giving an honest character reference, and that an employer should be able to rely on receiving one which was honest and truthful. It was equally important that the employee should be protected against an employer writing with malice something wicked or spiteful and likely to cause injury. The plaintiff rightly desired, if possible, to prevent any further doubtful references about her being given by the defendants, and this was of vital importance to her. On the other hand, it was equally vital that employers who honestly held certain opinions about a former employee should have the protection of the law in stating what was an honest opinion. He observed that the letter was written on an occasion of qualified privilege, and once this was established the law assumed that the writer had honestly believed the statements were true. Judgment was given to the defendants with costs.

Managers

Contracts with managerial personnel will usually contain additional or alternative provisions reflecting their greater responsibility. The terms of such a contract must not only make clear the scope of a manager's authority, but also specify any matters where he had no authority to bind his employer. An agreement might include provisions on the following lines:

1. The manager will devote the whole of his time to the company's business and use his best endeavours to extend the business.

2. He will be responsible for observing all orders and instructions from the company.

3. He must comply with all regulations laid down by statute and local bye-laws, and any breach or non-observance will be his sole responsibility.

4. He must take care of the company's property and effects.

5. He must keep proper accounts, stock records, and other information to comply with the law and the company's requirements.

6. Provisions about notice to terminate the contract, which may well be different from those applicable to other employees.

7. Any special provisions about limitations of his authority as to contracts he can make on behalf of the company, e.g. advertising.

Representative Occupation

An employee required by the terms of his employment to live in accommodation provided by his employer because it is necessary for the proper performance of his duties is not liable for assessment to income tax under Schedule E in respect thereof. If, however, his total emoluments exceed £5,000 a year (to be increased in the tax year 1978/9 to £7,500) he is liable for assessment in respect of heating, lighting, cleaning, etc. paid for by the employer in relation to the accommodation. Where an assessment is made, the basis will be the value of the benefits to the employee and not the cost to the employer. A full-time working director will be entitled to the tax benefit of representative occupation, irrespective of his emoluments, unless he has a substantial interest in the company.

EMPLOYER'S OTHER STATUTORY OBLIGATIONS

This chapter is concerned with legislation which may apply to some employers but not others, the principal statutes being the Shops Act and the Wages Councils Act. The following table shows the types of business affected:

	Shops	*Wages Council*
Club, registered		
residential	No	LR
non-residential	No	LNR
Hotel, guest house		
licensed	staff serving non-residents	LR—but not British Rail
unlicensed	No	No
Public House	Yes	LNR
Restaurant		
licensed	Yes	LR—but not British Rail
unlicensed	Yes	UPR

Where both Acts are applicable, it is important to note that, under the Shops Act, an employer must observe the conditions of the General Scheme unless he chooses to operate the Catering Trade Scheme. In either case he must allow his staff certain time off for meals, periods of rest, holidays, etc. with special rates applying to Sunday work. These obligations cannot be commuted for a money payment. While Wages Council regulations may cover similar matters their application must give an employee the benefit of the better conditions where they differ or conflict. Wages regulations now give longer holiday periods than the Shops Act and these apply instead of and not in addition to the Shops Act provisions.

The Wages Councils Act 1959

Most of the staff in the hotel and catering industry are subject to orders made under this Act. Wages Councils consist of equal numbers of representatives of employers and employees, together with some, usually three, independent members, one of whom acts as chairman. They meet to consider proposals for amending existing regulations and, after following established procedures designed to ensure adequate advance publicity and the consideration of any objections, may make an Order bringing new provisions about pay, holidays and other matters as from a specified date. As from that date, any employee employed on less favourable terms must receive any improvement due to him. The terms of a new order are, in effect, read into his contract of employment.

The employer's obligations are to pay employees not less than the *statutory minimum remuneration* specified in the appropriate order, clear of all deductions except those shown on page 49, to allow holidays and pay holiday remuneration when due not less than the order provides. There may be other provisions as well, such as guaranteed remuneration. An employer who fails to fulfil his obligations may be liable to a fine and any arrears due within the past three years. If necessary, a wages inspector may sue on behalf of an employee.

Permission may be given by a wages council for an employee affected by infirmity or physical incapacity, which renders him incapable of earning the statutory minimum remuneration, to be employed at a lower rate.

Gratuities, whether received individually by an employee, or put into a box (tronc) to be shared in agreed proportions later, are not the property of the employer. They belong unquestionably to the employees concerned.

Where a service charge is added to accounts as part of the contract between proprietor and guests or customers, it becomes his property and may be used towards the payment of wages. In order to avoid misunderstanding with the staff concerned, it is advisable to explain the situation on engagement and reach an agreement to form part of the contract of employment. The LR Wages Order recognises the service worker with a guarantee

EMPLOYER'S OTHER STATUTORY OBLIGATIONS

about gratuities by specifying a lower rate of minimum remuneration.

Employers are obliged to keep such records as are necessary to show that they have complied with the Act and the current order and such records must be kept for a period of three years. There is a further obligation to display the current order and any notices issued by a wages council so that employees concerned may be informed of the regulations affecting them. Failure to comply may involve a penalty on the employer or someone acting on his behalf (e.g. a manager) or both.

The Act provides for the appointment of inspectors to ensure compliance, and each inspector has a certificate of authority to act, which he must produce on demand to any person affected. An inspector may:

1. require information to be given about the pay, holidays and conditions of employment of any employee coming within the scope of the appropriate wages order;
2. question the employer and any employee concerned;
3. inspect records required to be kept by the employer;
4. enter at all reasonable times any premises where there are employees to whom a wages order applies.

An inspector may himself institute proceedings for any offence under the Act and may conduct such proceedings. He may also institute proceedings on behalf of an employee to recover any sum due from the employer. Anyone who obstructs an inspector may be liable to a penalty. Severe penalties apply where false records are knowingly maintained.

Orders made under the Act

Three types of business are currently covered by regulations:

Unlicensed Place of Refreshment (UPR)—cafes, tea shops, coffee and milk bars, snack bars, unlicensed restaurants.

Licensed Non-Residential Establishment (LNR)—public houses, licensed hotels and registered clubs with fewer than four letting bedrooms.

Licensed Residential Establishment and Licensed Restaurant (LR)—licensed hotels and registered clubs with four or more letting bedrooms or accommodation for eight or more guests, licensed restaurants, licensed holiday camps.

The former Industrial and Staff Canteen Undertakings Wages Council has been abolished, and there is no wages council for unlicensed hotels or guest houses.

The Shops Act 1950

Some employees in the catering industry are 'shop assistants' within the meaning of this Act, which superseded and consolidated various statutes from 1912 to 1938 and other legislation affecting shops. A 'shop' means any premises where retail trade or business is carried on, including the sale of refreshments and intoxicating (alcoholic) liquor. Employees likely to be concerned are those who work in a restaurant, cafe, public house, snack bar or tearoom, including waiting staff, kitchen staff and others directly or indirectly concerned in the service of customers.

An hotel or guest house serving residents only is not a shop, but if there is a room where non-residents are also accepted as a regular practice it would be regarded as a shop.

Employers with staff affected by the Act have a choice of two sets of conditions under which they may operate. There is the General Scheme, originally in the 1912 Act, which applies unless the alternative Catering Trade Scheme, originally in the 1913 Act, is chosen. The choice may be made annually and is indicated by the exhibition of a notice. The following details apply to persons of 18 years of age and over:

General Scheme	*Catering Trade Scheme*
Applicable to all persons wholly or mainly employed in a shop in connection with the serving of customers.	Applicable to all persons wholly or mainly employed in any capacity in the sale of refreshments for consumption on the premises.
A statutory half-holiday from 1.30 p.m. on one week-day must	No similar provision.

EMPLOYER'S OTHER STATUTORY OBLIGATIONS

General Scheme	*Catering Trade Scheme*
be allowed except in the week preceding a bank holiday.	
No maximum hours of work.	Maximum hours of work 65 per week excluding meal times.
Meal times: ¾ hour between 11.30 a.m. and 2.30 p.m. if meal taken on the premises, otherwise one hour. Tea ½ hour between 4 and 7 p.m.	Times not specified, but total ¾ hour if not employed after 3 p.m. Two hours where lunch and dinner service involved.
20 minutes break for rest in every 6 hours.	¾ hour break in every 6 hours.
For Sunday work exceeding four hours, a whole week-day off and no work on more than two other Sundays in same month.	26 whole Sundays off during the year, at least one in every three consecutive Sundays.
For work not exceeding four hours on a Sunday, a half-day's holiday from 1 p.m. on a week-day in the same or preceding week.	
These Sunday provisions do not apply to employees concerned with the sale of refreshments or liquor.	
Holiday provisions not specified.	32 whole week-days in each 12 months, with two half-days counting as a whole, starting not later than 3 p.m.

Inspectors appointed under the Act by local authorities make visits to premises concerned.

Employment of Young Persons

Legislation is contained in the Shops Act and also in the Young Persons (Employment) Act 1938, and employers have a choice as to the Act under which they prefer to operate. If the Shops Act is chosen, its provisions will apply to all young persons covered by both Acts. Adoption of the Catering Trade Scheme is automatic unless the employer chooses otherwise; a notice has to be exhibited if any arrangement for averaging hours over a fortnight applies. The main features of these Acts are:

Shops Act	Young Persons Act
Applicable to young persons wholly or mainly employed about the business of a shop, including any retail business not carried on in a shop, but excluding any young person employed in a residential hotel who is not a shop assistant.	Applicable to young persons employed in a residential hotel or club wholly or mainly in carrying messages, running errands or the reception of guests or members.

Maximum weekly working hours—

age 16-17	48 (96 per fortnight for maximum of 12 fortnights in a year, with no overtime).	48
under 16	44	44

Overtime—

age 16-17 maximum 50 hours per year, 8 per fortnight; none permitted under 16.	age 16-17 maximum 50 hours per year, 6 per week in not more than 12 weeks.

Intervals of rest—

½ hour in 6	½ hour in 5

Rest between duties—

11 consecutive hours between mid-day and mid-day; boys of 16-17 may serve meals from 10 p.m. to midnight	11 consecutive hours including 10 p.m. to 6 a.m.

Statutory half-holiday—

none	one week-day after 1 p.m.

Meals—	as for adults	¾ hour between 11.30 a.m. and 2.30 p.m.

Sunday work—

as for adults	none permitted unless whole day off given in same or preceding week.

For this purpose 'residential hotel' means premises used for the reception of guests or travellers desirous of dwelling or sleeping therein.

An employer must keep a record of the hours of employment, overtime, meal and rest intervals of every young person employed, or exhibit a notice specifying this information.

Employment in a bar
It is illegal to employ a young person in a bar (see page 100).

Offices Shops and Railway Premises Act 1953
This Act applies to premises or parts of premises within the scope of the Shops Act, such as restaurants and bars, and also to offices including offices in hotels, restaurants, public houses and similar premises, in which persons other than the immediate family of the proprietor are employed on clerical work, handling money and operating telephones. It does not apply to employees in the purely residential parts of hotels. The provisions of the Act may be superseded by regulations under the Health and Safety at Work Act.

The Act is concerned with:

Cleanliness of premises and equipment.

Overcrowding—except in rooms accessible to the public, employees must each have at least 40 sq. ft. of floor space and 400 c. ft. of air space.

Temperature—16°C (61°F) after first hour as a minimum, unless not reasonably practicable; thermometer to be available on every floor.

Ventilation—effective and suitable provision to be made.

Lighting—efficient and suitable, natural or artificial.

Sanitary conveniences—see SI 1964 No. 966..

Washing facilities—see SI 1964 No. 965.

Drinking water—adequate supply.

Accommodation for clothing—suitable and sufficient.

Sitting facilities—suitable facilities to be provided where there are opportunities without detriment to work.

Seats for sedentary work—for each person, to include footrest.

Eating facilities—suitable and sufficient where staff take meals on the premises.

Floors, passages and stairs—sound, safe, properly maintained.

Machinery—dangerous parts to be securely fenced or safety devices fitted; young persons not to clean if risk of injury from moving parts; persons using must be trained, see SI 1964 No. 971.

Heavy work is prohibited if likely to cause injury.

First aid—SI 1964 No. 970 specifies detailed requirements.

Fire precautions—restaurants now covered by Fire Precautions Act—offices to have fire certificate where more than 20 persons work at any one time, or more than 10 are employed elsewhere than on the ground floor; doors not to be fastened while staff are on the premises; contents of rooms not to obstruct access to means of escape; all exits to be conspicuously marked, fire alarm and fire-fighting equipment to be provided, and staff made familiar with means of escape.

Accidents—to be notified where loss of life or disablement for more than three days.

Information about the Act to be given to employees.

Enforcement—as regards fire precautions, by the fire authority, otherwise by the local authority.

Penalties for non-compliance may be imposed by a magistrates' court in England and Wales, or a sheriff court in Scotland.

Disabled Persons

Every employer with 20 or more employees is required to employ a certain number, or quota, of persons who have been registered as disabled. A disabled person is one who 'on account of injury, disease or congenital deformity is substantially handicapped' in getting and keeping suitable employment; this definition includes disablement from war service, industrial, road or other accident.

The obligation on these employers is to give employment to registered disabled persons up to a quota (at present 3%) of total staff. Failure to employ the quota does not constitute an offence.

EMPLOYER'S OTHER STATUTORY OBLIGATIONS 67

Vacancies in employment of passenger lift attendants and car park attendants must be appropriated to registered disabled persons only, if available.

FOOD

THE LAW AFFECTING CATERERS

The major Acts of concern to caterers are the Food and Drugs Act, 1955 (effective in England and Wales) and the Food and Drugs (Scotland) Act 1956. The principal provisions are:

1. Food offered for sale must be wholesome, and it is an offence to sell, offer or expose for sale, or to have in one's possession for purpose of sale, any food intended for but unfit for human consumption. It is a defence that, if the food is unfit because of some act or default of a supplier, the caterer can lay an information against that person; provided he had exercised due care, he might be acquitted.
2. Regulations may be made concerning the composition of food, including restrictions on the addition of harmful substances.
3. No person may lawfully sell to the prejudice of a purchaser any food which is not of the nature, or not of the substance, or not of the quality, demanded. For example, a request for bread and butter must be met with strict regard for the customer's wishes; to supply bread and margarine, or bread with a mixture of butter and margarine, without the customer's prior consent, would be an offence.
4. Any food for which a standard has been prescribed must not be sold or offered for sale unless it complies with that standard. The following are the principal foods of interest to caterers for which standards are at present in force:

Milk   Under the sale of milk regulations, an offence is committed if milk, other than separated or condensed milk, is knowingly sold which contains less than 3% of milk fat and less than 8.5% of milk solids other than milk fat. To comply with the regulations, therefore, milk must contain not more than 88.5% of water.

If hot milk, served as a beverage, is prepared by steam injection, care must be taken that the water content is not exceeded; in view of the difficulty of ensuring this, heating milk by steam injection cannot be recommended.

Butter Butter must be made exclusively from milk and must not contain more than 16% of water. It is an offence to sell as butter any mixture of butter with margarine or other fat not derived from milk.

Cream Regulations provide for the following standards:

(a) Cream, other than clotted cream, shall consist of that part of cow's milk rich in fat which has been separated by skimming or otherwise and no cream, whether described as cream, single cream, pouring cream, coffee cream, fruit cream, or as any other description of cream, shall contain less than 18% by weight of milk fat; half cream with 12% is now allowed.

(b) No sterilised cream shall contain less than 23% by weight of milk fat;

(c) No double cream or thick cream shall contain less than 48% by weight of milk fat;

(d) Clotted cream shall consist of that part of cow's milk rich in fat which has been produced and separated by the scalding, cooling and skimming of cow's milk or cream, and shall contain not less than 48% by weight of milk fat.

Cream substitutes It is an offence to sell or offer or expose for sale for human consumption;

(i) Any substance which resembles cream in appearance but is not cream, or

(ii) Any article of food containing such substance under a description or designation which includes the word 'cream' whether or not as part of a composite word.

The sale is permitted of the following so long as the description or designation of the substance does not mislead a purchaser into believing that it is cream:

THE LAW AFFECTING CATERERS

Reconstituted cream which, not being cream, resembles cream in appearance and contains no ingredient not derived from milk other than water or ingredients which may lawfully be contained in a substance sold for human consumption as cream;

Imitation cream which, not being cream or reconstituted cream, resembles cream in appearance and is produced by emulsifying edible oils or fats with water either by themselves or with other substances not prohibited by regulations.

Ice Cream Regulations prescribe compositional requirements for dairy ice cream (otherwise known as dairy cream ice or cream ice), milk ice, Parev ice (Kosher ice) and other ice cream. There are provisions about labelling, advertisement and description (e.g. on menus).

Other Food Standards There are regulations controlling the composition, labelling and description of various foods including fish cakes, meat pies, sausage rolls, sausages and other meat products, and canned meat. Where controlled items are purchased from suppliers (e.g. sausages and canned meat) the supplier should be asked to confirm compliance with requirements. Good culinary practice will normally be sufficient to ensure compliance where controlled items are made on the premises, e.g. fish cakes.

HYGIENE

Regulations made under the respective Food and Drugs Acts apply throughout Great Britain to every place where food is handled in connection with a trade or business, including shops, hotels, restaurants, guest houses, canteens and clubs, as well as institutions such as schools and hospitals. The following matters are covered:

Premises—insanitary premises must not be used and it is an offence to expose food to the risk of contamination.

Cleanliness—articles of equipment used in food handling must be constructed in such a way that they can easily be kept clean, and must be kept clean.

Personal cleanliness—food handlers must keep themselves and their clothing as clean as possible, and cover any open cut or sore with a suitable waterproof dressing. They must not handle food while suffering from infection likely to cause food poisoning, and the person carrying on the business must immediately notify the local medical officer of health if an employee reports illness of this kind.

Smoking, spitting and the use of snuff are prohibited while handling food.

Washing facilities must be provided and maintained for employees, including hot and cold water, or water at a controlled temperature, soap, nail-brushes and clean towels or other drying facilities.

First aid materials to be kept in a place readily accessible.

Overclothing, sufficient, clean and washable, to be worn by handlers of open (unprotected) food, other than raw vegetables; this regulation does not apply to waiting staff.

Protection from contamination—food likely to provide a good medium for the growth of disease organisms, e.g. consisting of or containing meat, fish, gravy, egg or milk, must be kept at a suitable temperature to prevent multiplication of bacteria. Regulations specify a temperature of above 62.7°C (145°F) or below 10°C (50°F). Various items containing these ingredients are exempted. Food which is exposed for sale, or which is kept available for replenishing such food, is also exempted subject to certain conditions.

Soil drainage systems—air intakes must not be in a food room, and every inlet must be trapped.

Cisterns supplying water to food rooms must not supply sanitary conveniences except with efficient flushing apparatus.

Sanitary conveniences must not be in a food room, or in a position where odours can penetrate to a food room; they must be kept clean and in efficient order; a notice must be displayed to encourage washing of hands.

THE LAW AFFECTING CATERERS

Water supply to be clean and wholesome, and constantly available.

Accommodation for outdoor clothing—suitable and sufficient lockers or cupboards to be provided for outdoor clothing and footwear not worn during working hours.

Washing of food and equipment—suitable facilities to be provided.

Lighting and ventilation to be suitable and sufficient; no food room may be used for *sleeping* or communicate with a bedroom.

Walls, floors, doors, windows, ceilings must be kept clean, and in good order to prevent as far as reasonably practicable infestation by rats, mice and insects.

Refuse—adequate space to be provided, suitably sited, with accumulation in a food room kept to practicable minimum.

The regulations are administered by local authorities. They are authorised to grant certificates of exemption from compliance with certain regulations concerning structure of premises; there is a right of appeal to a magistrates' court (sheriff court in Scotland) against the refusal or withdrawal of a certificate.

There are penalties for offences against the Act or the regulations, and a person against whom proceedings are taken may have any other person he alleges to have caused the offence brought before the court. If the court considers an offence sufficiently grave it may disqualify the offender from using his premises for a period of up to two years on the application of the local authority. Before such an order can be made, the offender must be given not less than 14 days' notice before the date of the hearing that application for such an order is to be made.

The Food and Drugs (Control of Food Premises) Act 1976 empowers a local authority to apply to a court for an emergency closure order after three days' notice if it believes there is imminent danger to health. Where a closure order is made, the local authority must specify the measures required to be taken to remove the danger. If a court subsequently decides that, at the relevant time, there was no danger to health, the proprietor of the premises may claim compensation for any loss from the local authority.

Damage by Pests

The Prevention of Damage by Pests Act 1949 requires local authorities to take all steps necessary to ensure that persons engaged in food businesses take adequate measures to keep their premises free from rats, mice and other pests. Occupiers of all premises infested by rats are obliged to report the fact to the authority and to arrange for the vermin to be destroyed.

Inspectors from the Department of Agriculture have right of entry to the premises of caterers (among others) and provision is made in the Act for restrictions on the sale or use of food or equipment in infested premises, destruction of attacked food, structural alteration to premises to combat attacks by vermin. There are heavy penalties.

Kitchen Waste

Collectors of kitchen waste have to be licensed by the Department of Agriculture, Fisheries and Food, licences being granted only to those who have proper facilities for sterilisation.

THE SALE OF LIQUOR

THE LICENSING SYSTEM—England and Wales

Licensing by local justices began on 1st May 1552 with an Act requiring keepers of alehouses to be bound by recognisance. It provided for the issue by two justices of a licence to carry on the trade, and although it was repealed in 1829, its principles survive to-day in the Licensing Act 1964.

Licensing Authorities
In each licensing district, a committee of magistrates is appointed to act in licensing matters. They hold an annual meeting in the first fortnight of February, and not less than four nor more than eight transfer sessions at regular intervals throughout the year. The annual meeting may be held on different days for different parts of the district and at more than one place.

Powers exercisable only at the annual meeting include:
> (a) The renewal of justices' licences;
> (b) The making of regulations to restrict repeated applications for transfers or special removals;
> (c) Fixing the general licensing hours for the district.

Types of Licence
Application can be made for one of the following justices' licences:
> On-Licence: for sale of all, or some, classes of liquor for consumption either on or off the premises. The classes are:
>> (i) Intoxicating liquor of all descriptions;
>> (ii) Beer, cider and wine;
>> (iii) Beer and cider;

(iv) Cider;
(v) Wine.

Off-Licence: for sale for consumption off the premises of
(i) Intoxicating liquor of all descriptions, or
(ii) Beer, cider and wine.

Residential Licence: for sale only to residents and their private friends;

Restaurant Licence: for sale only to persons taking substantial meals on the premises;

Residential and Restaurant Licence: a combination of the two foregoing.

The last three are also known as Part IV licences—sections 93 to 101 of the Act.

How to Apply for a Justices' Licence

The procedure an applicant has to follow is:

1. Not less than 21 days before the application is made, give notice of his intention to apply to:
   (a) the clerk to the licensing justices, enclosing a plan of the premises to be licensed;
   (b) the chief officer of police;
   (c) the appropriate local authority;
   (d) the fire authority.

2. Within 28 days before the application is made, cause notice of his application to be displayed for a period of seven days in a place where it can conveniently be read by the public on or near the premises to be licensed;

3. Not more than 28 days and not less than 14 days before the application is made, and on such day or days as may be fixed by the licensing justices, advertise notice of the application in a local newspaper.

Notices must give the name and address of the applicant, his trade or calling during the six months preceding the giving of the notice, a description of the licence for which he intends to apply and a description of the situation of the premises; these notices may be signed by the applicant or his authorised agent. Where an applicant, through inadvertence or misadventure, fails to comply with these requirements, the justices may, on such terms as they think fit, postpone consideration of the application, and when the terms have been complied with may consider the application later.

Disqualified Persons
The following persons are disqualified from holding a licence:
  1. An officer executing legal process of court, while holding such office;
  2. Any person convicted of forging or using a forged justices' licence knowing it to have been forged (disqualified for life);
  3. Any holder of a justices' licence convicted for allowing licensed premises to be used as a brothel (disqualified for life);
  4. Any person ordered to be disqualified on conviction for selling liquor without a justices' licence (for a first offence the period of disqualification is stated in the order, a second conviction involves disqualification for life);
  5. A licensed pilot;
  6. Any person disqualified under any other Act.

Hearing of Application
An applicant for a new licence, if so required by the justices, must attend in person, and an application may be postponed until he does attend.

In the case of an application for a new on-licence, the justices must take into account public need, and any member of the community may, without notice, oppose the grant of a new licence on public grounds or on any interest of his own. When hearing an application for a residential or restaurant licence, the justices are not concerned with public need.

In the case of a residential licence, the applicant must satisfy the justices that the premises are *bona fide* used or intended to be used for the purpose of habitually providing for reward board and lodging, including breakfast and either lunch or dinner or both. Unless in particular circumstances the justices dispense with the condition, a room with adequate sitting accommodation must be provided on the premises in which no liquor may be supplied or consumed, and this room must not be a bedroom or dining room.

The applicant for a restaurant licence must satisfy the justices that the premises are structurally adapted and *bona fide* used or intended to be used for the purpose of habitually providing the customary main meal at midday or in the evening or both.

The justices cannot refuse to grant a residential or restaurant licence if the foregoing conditions are satisfied, except on the following grounds:

(a) The applicant is not of full age, or in some other respect is not a fit and proper person to hold a licence;

(b) The premises are not suitable for the purpose;

(c) A large proportion of the persons residing at or frequenting the premises, is habitually made up of young persons under 18 unaccompanied by an adult;

(d) Within the preceding 12 months a justices' on-licence for the premises has been forfeited, or the premises have been ill-conducted under a justices' on-licence or a refreshment house licence;

(e) If any other conditions (see page 83) are not satisfied or if there is self-service of liquor.

Where justices refuse an application for a new on-licence, other than a Part IV licence, they can at the request of the applicant treat his application as being for a residential and/or restaurant licence as the case may be. If they still refuse they are obliged to state their reasons in writing.

There is an appeal to a Crown Court against the grant or refusal of a licence. Only objectors who appeared before the justices are entitled to appeal against the grant of an ordinary on-licence, but an applicant may appeal against conditions attached or against a refusal. On an appeal against the grant of a licence, the applicant for the licence and not the licensing justices will be the respondent. On an appeal against a refusal to grant a licence, any person who opposed the grant will be respondent as well as the justices. Where a Crown Court grants or confirms the grant of a licence, it may attach such conditions as the licensing justices might have attached, and the licence comes into force on the disposal of the appeal.

The Grant of a Licence

A licence is granted to one or more individuals in respect of particular premises. If the premises are occupied by a tenant the licence is granted to him and not to the landlord. Where a corporate body (e.g. a company) is concerned, the licence may be in the name of a director, secretary or other official, either alone or with the manager of the premises. There is no legal reason why a minor or a woman should not be granted a licence, but justices usually refuse licences to a minor, and some justices insist on a man as licence-holder if the circumstances and situation of the premises warrant this.

The justices no longer have discretion to attach conditions to an on-licence so as to prohibit a bar. In the case of a Part IV licence, there is a statutory requirement that beverages other than intoxicating liquor, including drinking water, must be available, and renewal may be refused if this condition is not complied with.

The holder of an on-licence or the applicant for a new licence may ask for a condition to be attached to provide that at certain times of the year there shall be no permitted hours in the premises, and the justices if satisfied that the requirements of the district make it desirable may attach such a condition. The licence will then be known as a seasonal licence. The condition may be varied at the request of the person applying for renewal, transfer or removal of the licence.

Where a licence is granted in respect of premises open only for lunch or dinner, a condition may be attached limiting the permitted hours to the lunch period or the dinner period.

An applicant may ask for a licence to be a six-day licence or an early-closing licence (involving closing one hour earlier than the usual time).

Justices' licences run from 5th April, and a new licence has effect from the time of the grant (except when there is an appeal) until the end of the licensing year, or if granted between 5th January and 5th April until the end of the following licensing year.

Structure of Premises

The justices have some control over the structure of licensed premises. Any alterations proposed to be made to on-licensed premises which give increased drinking facilities in a public or common part of the premises, or conceal from observation a public or common part of the premises used for drinking, or affect communication between the public part where liquor is sold and the remainder of the premises and any street or public way, must be approved by the licensing justices. There is no appeal against refusal of approval. A public part is one open to non-residents; a common part is one open to residents or a particular class of them. Internal communications must not be made between any licensed premises and any other premises used for public entertainment or resort or as a refreshment house.

If unauthorised alterations are made, the licence may be forfeited on order of a court of summary jurisdiction, or the court may require the premises to be restored to their original condition within a given time. If forfeiture of licence is ordered, the owner of the premises may apply for a protection order.

Alterations required by a local authority do not come within these provisions. The authority has power under the Public Health Acts to require by notice the occupier of an inn, public house, beerhouse or refreshment house to provide and maintain a reasonable number of sanitary conveniences.

The justices have power to require structural alterations to be made within the limits mentioned before granting a renewal of licence. They have no control over the structure of off-licensed premises.

Provisional Grant of a New Licence

Where new premises are about to be constructed or are in the course of construction, or existing premises are about to be altered or extended for the purpose of the sale of liquor, whether for consumption on or off the premises, persons interested may make application for a provisional grant in respect of such premises, and the licensing justices may grant a provisional licence if satisfied with the plans, or a plan sufficient to identify the site and a description of the premises.

A provisional grant is not valid until declared final by order of the licensing justices, made after proper notice has been given, and subject to no objection as to the character of the provisional licensee. The same notices are required as for a new licence, and the declaration of finality is in effect the grant of a new licence.

Register of Licences
It is the duty of the clerk to the licensing justices to keep a register of licences granted in the district. The register contains a list of the premises concerned, the name of the owner, the holder of the licence for the time being, and details of any offence committed by the licence-holder. Any ratepayer, licence-holder or owner of licensed premises in the district may inspect the register on payment of a fee; police officers may inspect without payment.

Renewal
The occupier of the licensed premises at the time of the annual meeting is the person entitled to apply for the renewal of the licence. No formal notice is necessary and the applicant need not attend unless specially requested. In some areas one application may be made by a local association on behalf of its members; otherwise application should be made by letter. Inadvertent omission to apply can usually be remedied on certain conditions.

No objection to a renewal can be entertained unless written notice is given and served on the licence-holder who is applying for renewal, not less than seven days before the meeting, stating in general terms the grounds of objection. At the meeting objection may be made without notice, whereupon the grant of the renewal may be adjourned for the attendance of the licence-holder. In hearing an opposed application, the justices may not receive any evidence not given on oath.

Licensing justices may require a plan of the premises to be submitted on application for a renewal and can order structural alterations to be made within a given time. There is an appeal to a Crown Court against such an order. If an order is made and complied with, no further requisition may be made for five years. A fine may be imposed for non-compliance.

A renewal can only be granted where the licence is in force at the date of the meeting or was in force at the date of the last meeting. The term 'renewal' applies only to the continuance of the licence on the existing basis; restrictions can only be removed by applying for a new licence (but see page 83 for varying them). There is an appeal to a Crown Court against a refusal to renew; if the licence expires before the appeal is heard, the licensing justices or the Crown Court may permit the applicant to carry on business.

Old Beerhouse Licences

Some special provisions apply to the renewal of beerhouse licences in force on 1st May 1869, known as ante-1869 beerhouses, 'old beerhouses' or protected licences. Renewal without compensation can be refused only on the following grounds:

1. Where the applicant has failed to produce evidence of good character;
2. Where the house is of a disorderly character or any adjacent premises owned or occupied by the applicant are of such a character;
3. Where the applicant has forfeited a licence or been disqualified;
4. Where the applicant or the house is not qualified as required by law; or on the general ground that the applicant is not a fit and proper person.

Refusal on any other ground justified a reference to the compensation authority; compensation in these cases is usually at a higher rate than for other licensed premises.

Old On-licences

This description means licences in force on 15th August 1904. With the exception of a licence for wine only, the justices may refuse renewal on any of the following grounds, without compensation:

1. Where the premises are ill-conducted or structurally unsuitable. The justices are deemed to refuse renewal for the former reason where the licence-holder has persistently and

unreasonably refused to supply suitable refreshment other than liquor at a reasonable price or has failed to fulfil any reasonable undertaking given to the justices on grant or previous renewal. The justices may ask an applicant to give an undertaking as to the conduct of the business, but cannot compel him to do so, but may adjourn so that the registered owner of the premises may have an opportunity to be heard;

2. Where the proposed holder of the licence is not a suitable person;

3. Where renewal of the licence would be void, i.e. if granted to a disqualified person or in respect of disqualified premises.

Power to refuse renewal on other grounds is vested in the compensation authority, which can act only on a reference from the justices.

If renewal is not refused but the question requires consideration, the justices grant a provisional renewal and refer to the compensation authority. If that authority refuses renewal compensation becomes payable.

Licensing justices have discretion to refuse renewal of licences granted since 15th August 1904 on any ground without compensation, but there is an appeal to a Crown Court.

Transfer

The applicant for the transfer to him of a licence in the name of someone else must, at least 21 days before a licensing sessions, serve notices on the same persons as for a new licence and also on the present holder, if any. Notices should give the name of the person to whom the licence is to be transferred, his residence and his trade or calling during the past six months. Both the applicant and the present holder, if still alive, must attend unless the justices dispense with attendance, and any agreement between the parties as to the transfer must be produced. Anyone may oppose the application, no notice being necessary. If the matter is one of urgency, the proper course is to apply to a court of summary jurisdiction for a Protection Order.

The intended transferee must be a fit and proper person, and it is the duty of the police to make enquiries as to his character.

Transfers can be granted only in certain circumstances and to certain persons but the licence need not be in force at the time; the following list covers the principal cases:

Death of licence-holder—his personal representative or the new tenant or occupier;

Incapacity of licence-holder to carry on business owing to illness or infirmity—his assigns or the new tenant or occupier;

Bankruptcy of licence-holder—his trustee or the new tenant or occupier;

Occupation of premises given up or about to be given up by licence-holder—new tenant or occupier, or *bona fide* new owner;

Wilful omission or neglect of occupier to apply for renewal—new tenant or occupier;

Where a licence has been forfeited by reason of personal act of licence-holder and another person has obtained a protection order—the owner or any person applying on his behalf; a transfer may be granted as if licence was still valid.

Licensing justices can refuse the transfer of an off-licence, or of an on-licence granted since 1904; there is an appeal to a Crown Court.

A transfer takes effect from the date of the grant until the 5th April following.

Protection Order

Where circumstances arise in which a transfer of licence becomes necessary pending the next sessions, application can be made for a protection order, which is a temporary authority or provisional transfer enabling business to be carried on until the licence is transferred or removed. Where a licence has been forfeited or the holder becomes disqualified, the owner of the premises or a person authorised by him may be granted a protection order.

At least one week's notice must be served by the applicant on the chief officer of police; notice is similar to that required in the case of a transfer. In urgent cases, the notice can be dispensed with on good grounds. Special provisions apply in London; in other districts a protection order may be granted by a court of summary jurisdiction. An order confers on the holder the same rights and obligations as the justices' licence in force or last in force for the premises.

A protection order is not necessary in the case of heirs, executors, administrators or assigns of a deceased licence-holder, or the trustee in bankruptcy of a licence-holder; they carry on business until the next sessions but one.

Removal
The transfer of a licence from one premises to another is termed a Removal, and removals can be ordinary or special:

(a) An Ordinary Removal is a transfer of licence, other than a Part IV licence, on any ground other than that of a special removal; a licence, either on or off, may be removed for any good reason without limitation as to area, application being made to the licensing justices of the district to which it is desired to remove the licence.

(b) A Special Removal is a transfer of an *old on-licence* from one premises to another in the same licensing district where:

(i) The premises for which a licence has been granted are or are about to be pulled down or occupied under any Act for the improvement of highways, or for any other public purpose; or

(ii) The premises have been rendered unfit for use for the business there carried on under the licence by reason of fire, tempest, or other unforeseen and unavoidable calamity.

Application for a removal can be made at any licensing sessions by the person desiring to be the licence-holder when the licence is removed.

Occasional Licence
An Occasional Licence may be granted by licensing justices to a person already holding an on-licence to sell the same kinds of liquor for which he is licensed at premises other than his own. The holder of a residential licence is not entitled to apply, and the

holder of a restaurant licence may apply only where the sale of liquor is to be ancillary to the supply of substantial refreshment. These licences are intended for dinners, balls, fairs, race-meetings, exhibitions and other functions on unlicensed premises.

Application has to be made to a petty sessional court. Where at least a month's notice can be given, application can be made by post to the clerk and, unless the justices so require, personal appearance is not necessary. In other cases, notice of intention to apply must be served on the superintendent of police at least 24 hours before the application is due to be made, giving the name and address of the applicant, the place and occasion, period and hours for which the licence is required. If there is no sitting of the petty sessional court within three days before the licence is required two justices sitting together may act.

An occasional licence cannot be granted for Christmas Day, Good Friday or any day appointed for public fast or thanksgiving or for any Sunday in parts of Wales having no permitted hours. The period of any one licence may not exceed three weeks, and the hours for which it is granted must be specified.

Justices who contended that the word 'occasional' constituted a complete bar to the granting of applications made regularly were over-ruled by the High Court which decided that justices had complete discretion.

The premises become licensed premises for the period specified and the usual rules governing good conduct must be observed.

The Compensation Scheme

The Licensing Act 1904 set up a mutual insurance compensation scheme to provide compensation for owners of licensed premises in existence on 15th August 1904 which are subsequently declared redundant. Compensation authorities are appointed for one or more licensing districts, and they control Compensation Funds derived from any charges made on all old on-licensed premises in the area, other than those licensed for the sale of wine only. If an authority decides not to make any charges it

THE LICENSING SYSTEM

notifies the Home Secretary; where charges are imposed they are payable on renewal of the licence.

A compensation authority cannot take away a licence or give compensation except in cases referred to it by the licensing justices. Reference to the authority must be on some ground other than one on which refusal to renew without compensation could be made. Transfer applications can be referred to the authority if the justices wish the licence to be taken away.

Where a compensation authority has any case to consider, it must hold three meetings: a preliminary meeting, a principal meeting and a supplemental meeting. The first must be held before the end of May, to consider reports from licensing justices, having regard to the funds available, the circumstances and needs of the area. If the authority decides not to proceed in any particular case, the licence is regarded as renewed. Otherwise, the hearing of interested parties is fixed for the principal meeting.

Not less than fourteen days' notice of the principal meeting must be published and notice must be sent to the licensee and the registered owner of the premises concerned. The authority may hear evidence on oath, and can act judicially only on such evidence. The proceedings are open to the public; there is no appeal but the authority may state a case for the High Court.

The supplemental meeting is called to ascertain the persons entitled to compensation, and to approve the amount to be paid and its division among them. After the principal meeting, 21 days' notice must be given in two local newspapers requesting claims from interested persons. The amount of compensation is the difference between the value of the premises and their value when unlicensed, plus a sum for depreciation of fixtures arising from refusal to renew the licence. If no agreement can be reached, the amount is determined by the Inland Revenue, and is subject to an appeal to the High Court.

The licence concerned ceases to have effect at the expiration of seven days after the date fixed for payment of compensation money. In the case of prolonged delay a renewal is granted.

THE CONDUCT OF LICENSED PREMISES—
England and Wales

Name of licence-holder to be displayed
The full name of the holder of a justices' licence (other than a residential licence) must be displayed in a conspicuous place on the licensed premises as directed by the justices, stating whether the licence is 'on' or 'off', the liquor which may be sold, and if appropriate whether the licence is a six-day or early-closing licence. In the case of a restaurant licence, it is sufficient if the notice indicates that the holder is licensed to sell for consumption on the premises with meals.

'Entry' with Excise
A licensee, if required by the Commissioners of Customs and Excise, must make 'entry' with the Excise of every building, room, cellar or other place intended to be used for keeping liquor, distinguishing each place or thing by a separate letter or number. A retailer of spirits may be required to make entry of all casks, vessels and utensils to be used for keeping spirits.

Meetings on licensed premises
The following meetings must not be held on licensed premises:
　　1. Coroner's inquest (but only where other suitable premises are available;
　　2. Local government meetings;
　　3. Meetings concerned with parliamentary or local government elections.

Exceptions to these rules apply where a part of licensed premises is ordinarily let for public meetings, but there must be a separate entrance and no access by the public to the part where liquor is on sale.

Residence on premises
The licensee is not required by law to reside on his licensed premises, though the justices may make such a condition. He is not obliged to notify the police when he is on holiday.

Permitted Hours
There are no closing hours for on-licensed premises and nothing to prevent them being open at any time, but there must be no sale or consumption of liquor on the premises outside 'permitted hours' except as mentioned hereafter.

Permitted hours are fixed for each district by the licensing justices at the annual meeting, within limits set out in the 1964 Act and subject to certain variations which the Act allows. There is no statutory obligation on a licensee to keep his premises open during the whole of the permitted hours.

Week-days
The general permitted hours on week-days, other than Christmas Day and Good Friday, are the nine hours from 11 a.m. to 3 p.m. and 5.30 to 10.30 p.m. In London, there are 9½ permitted hours ending at 11 p.m., and outside London the justices may extend the hours to 9½ ending at 11 p.m. if satisfied that the requirements of the district make it desirable (e.g. holiday resorts). The justices may vary the general hours so that they begin not earlier than 10 a.m., with a single break of not less than two hours in the afternoon, so long as the total hours do not exceed 9 or 9½ and the terminal hour is not earlier than 10.30 p.m. Where the mid-day hours end before 3 p.m., service of drinks with meals may take place until that time in approved premises.

Justices may vary the hours so as to provide for the whole year, or for periods of not less than eight weeks, and may fix different hours for different week-days.

The reference to London is to the 'Metropolis' which is the Inner London area and the City of London.

Approved premises are those qualifying for a supper hour certificate.

Sundays

In England, the permitted hours on Sundays, Christmas Day and Good Friday are the 5½ hours from 12 noon to 2 p.m. and 7 to 10.30 p.m., but drinks may be served with meals up to 3 p.m. in approved premises.

In Wales local polls may be requested to determine the Sunday opening of public houses at intervals of seven years, the next being due in 1982. The present position is that 31 out of 37 districts have voted for Sunday opening, the six 'dry' districts being parts of Gwynedd and Dyfed including Anglesey. These polls do not affect registered clubs.

Variation of Permitted Hours

There are a number of ways in which permitted hours in individual premises may be varied by application to the following:

> In the City of London—The Commissioner of City Police (subject to the approval of the Lord Mayor);
>
> In the Metropolitan Police District—The Commissioner of Police for the Metropolis (subject to the approval of the Home Secretary);
>
> Elsewhere in England and Wales—a petty sessional court.

General Order of Exemption

Where it can be shown to be necessary to provide for persons attending a public market or following a lawful calling outside permitted hours (e.g. newspaper production) application can be made by licensees in the immediate vicinity for exemption on certain days and during specified hours. A notice stating the days and hours during which premises are permitted to be open must be exhibited outside. The authority may alter the order or withdraw it, otherwise it remains in operation indefinitely.

Special Order of Exemption

A licensee may be permitted to sell liquor during an extended period (afternoon or evening) on a 'special occasion', e.g. a wedding reception, dinner, ball or other similar function held on licensed premises. The authority has absolute discretion as to what constitutes a special occasion and there is no appeal against refusal of an order. There is no legal bar to an extension being granted in respect of a Sunday or on Christmas Day, except on Sunday to the holder of a six-day licence.

An order has the effect of extending the hours for the whole premises, but the justices will usually ask for an undertaking that sales during the extended period are confined to persons attending the function.

Application may be made by post on the same conditions as for an occasional licence.

Supper Hour Certificate

Application may be made by a licensee for an extension of permitted hours in the evenings for the sale of liquor with meals. Notice must be sent at least one week before a licensing sessions to the superintendent of police and the clerk to the licensing justices. The justices must be satisfied that the premises are structurally adapted and *bona fide* used or intended to be used for habitually providing substantial refreshment to which the supply of liquor is ancillary. These are the only factors the justices may take into account.

The holder of a restaurant licence is entitled to this certificate as his licence already serves as approval of premises for this purpose.

The licensee must give not less than fourteen days' notice in writing to the police of his intention to use this facility and the date this will take effect. A notice must be permanently affixed in a conspicuous place to the effect that the certificate applies; its application will continue indefinitely unless at least fourteen days' notice is given to the police before the expiration of a licensing year.

The grant of this certificate has the effect of adding one hour to the evening permitted hours on week-days and Sundays, except in parts of Wales without Sunday opening. The extra hour applies to the part of the premises set apart for the service of meals, and any bar in that part of the premises may remain open for the service of drinks to persons taking table meals; elsewhere all ordinary drinking bars must be closed during the extra hour, and no supply made except for consumption at a meal supplied at the same time in that part of the premises where meals are usually served.

The certificate also serves as approval of premises in a district where normal permitted hours end earlier than 3 p.m., enabling drinks to be served with meals up to that hour, after notice has been given to the police.

What constitutes 'a meal' has not been defined, but justices expect a meal to be substantial to comply with this provision, and may specify a minimum charge for such a meal or stipulate that the ordinary charges for meals must apply. A sandwich, unless substantial, is not likely to be regarded as sufficient.

Extended Hours Order

This order enables drinks to be supplied with meals up to 1 a.m. on week-days where musical or other entertainment is regularly provided on every day or on certain days in each week, beginning well before the end of normal licensing hours. The premises must qualify for a supper hour certificate. Liquor must not be supplied during the extra time when entertainment is not provided, or after the time when entertainment or the provision of substantial refreshment has ended; supply must not be made to any person admitted to the premises after midnight or less than half-an-hour before the entertainment is due to end. For this purpose 'entertainment' means performance by persons actually present and performing. An order may be granted for part of the year for not less than four weeks, and does not apply on Good Friday, nor after midnight on Maundy Thursday and Easter Eve.

Application is made by the licensee after giving notice to the same persons and at the same times as for a new licence. As this is an order and not a certificate, the justices have discretion as to a grant. When a grant is made, fourteen days' written notice must be given to the police, and a notice displayed in the part of the premises concerned.

Special Hours Certificate

Where music and dancing are provided as well as substantial refreshment, a special hours certificate may be granted permit-

THE CONDUCT OF LICENSED PREMISES

ting the sale of liquor as an ancillary to a meal. The premises must be in an area subject to statutory regulations (see page 117) and the facilities must be provided on every week-day or on particular week-days in every week, and the certificate applies only when they are provided.

A notice, signed by the applicant or his agent, must be sent to the police and the clerk to the justices at least one week before applying for a certificate. The justices must grant the certificate if the conditions have been met and, after the grant, fourteen days' notice to bring it into effect or to discontinue it must be given to the police.

The certificate has the effect of making the evening permitted hours 6.30 p.m. to 2 a.m. (3 a.m. in London); the permitted hours cease between midnight and 2 a.m. (3 a.m. in London) if music and dancing stop. The certificate does not apply to Sundays, except that it continues the Saturday hours into Sunday; it includes Christmas Day when not a Sunday, but does not include Good Friday, and permitted hours end at midnight on Maundy Thursday and Easter Eve. The certificate may, and usually does, apply to part of the premises only.

Originally sale at bars was not allowed but that restriction has now been removed. A notice that a certificate is in force must be exhibited. A certificate may be granted for part of the year. There is provision for revocation if conditions are not complied with or if disorderly conduct takes place.

Exceptions to Permitted Hours

Apart from the above-mentioned special arrangements for the extension of permitted hours, there are a number of exceptions to the rule that no sale or consumption may take place outside normal permitted hours. These exceptions are:

Drinking-up time Ten minutes are allowed at the end of each term of permitted hours for consumption.

Residents Sale to and consumption by a resident on licensed premises may take place at any time, and a resident may entertain his non-resident private friends at any time at his own expense. Residents must be *bona fide* resident and it is not sufficient merely to enter names in the register. The licensee has no duty to see that non-residents leave hotel lounges at the end of drinking-up time, and if many non-residents frequent the hotel it may be preferable to serve residents after permitted hours in a part of the premises to which non-residents do not have access.

Supply with meals Consumption by non-residents, other than private friends of residents, may take place with a meal within half-an-hour after permitted hours, provided the liquor was supplied during permitted hours as an ancillary to the meal. This provision applies both to the afternoon and evening conclusion of permitted hours, including the hours as extended by a supper hour certificate, an extended hours order or a special hours certificate.

Licensee's friends and staff
The licence-holder may entertain his private friends at any time, and also his staff, providing in both cases that the entertainment is at his own expense. The person carrying on the business, if not the holder of the licence, may also do so.

Off-consumption
In premises licensed for sale for consumption off the premises, the permitted hours on week-days begin at 8.30 a.m. and there is no afternoon break. Where premises are 'on' and 'off' licensed, these permitted hours apply only to a part set aside for off-sales having a separate entrance with no access by the public to the on-licensed part.

Closing for the winter
There is no statutory prohibition against the closure of licensed premises during a part of the year. If all facilities, including bars, are closed and the licensee cannot produce adequate reasons for his action, he runs the risk of losing his licence when renewal becomes due on the ground that it is not required to meet the needs of the public. As an alternative, he can apply for a seasonal licence.

SALE OF LIQUOR
The duties of a licensee with regard to the sale of liquor include the following:

THE CONDUCT OF LICENSED PREMISES

1. He must not serve liquor for which he is not licensed.
2. If his licence restricts sales to certain persons, he must not sell to other persons.
3. If he is an hotel proprietor, he has an obligation to serve respectable travellers; if he is not, he may choose whom he will serve and need not give a reason for a refusal.
4. The sale of liquor in a bar to a person under 18 is prohibited. It is an offence for a licensee *knowingly* to sell or allow sale, and also an offence for anyone to purchase with the intention that the liquor is to be consumed by a person under 18. The word 'knowingly' does not oblige a licensee to ask a young person's age, but makes it desirable to exhibit a notice so that customers are aware of the law. The licensee needs to ensure that his employees observe the law in his absence.

Beer or cider may be served to a person over 16 for consumption at a meal in a place set aside for meals, not being an open bar.

The licensee or his employee must not knowingly deliver to a person under 18 any liquor for consumption off the premises except at his residence or working-place. No one may knowingly send a person under 18 to obtain liquor from licensed premises, but a member of the licensee's family or staff under 18 may act as messenger to deliver liquor.

5. Pre-packed liquor, other than wine, must be marked with an indication of quantity, except where the quantity is less than 3 fluid ounces or more than one gallon.

Draught beer and cider may be sold only in quantities of one-third of a pint, half a pint or a multiple of half a pint, except where either is a constituent of a mixture of two or more liquids.

The sale of open carafe wine is only permitted in the following quantities: 25, 50, 75 and 100 centilitres, 10 and 20 fluid ounces. The quantities offered must be stated on the wine list. Legislation is awaited concerning sale of wine by the glass.

Sale, otherwise than in bottle, of gin, rum, vodka and whisky (but not brandy) is allowed only in quantities of one-quarter (4-out), one-fifth (5-out) or one-sixth (6-out) of a gill (5 fluid ounces). Only one measure may be used for all these spirits at any one point of sale, and a notice must be displayed stating which measure is in use. Exceptions to this rule are sales of any of these liquors as a constituent of a mixture of three or more liquids, and also in a mixture of two liquids made up in other quantities at the express wish of the customer.

All measures must be stamped by a weights and measures authority.

6. Licensees are required to make known to prospective customers the prices of all drinks exposed for sale by retail for consumption on the premises, both alcoholic and non-alcoholic. Prices must be clearly legible before ordering. Cocktails prepared individually at a customer's request are exempted. Mixed drinks may be priced as mixtures or as a combination of constituents. The local weights and measures authority is responsible for enforcement.

7. There must be no sale on credit to a non-resident for consumption on the premises, but supply with a meal may be paid for on the bill for the meal. A resident in an hotel may pay for drinks, whether served with a meal or not, with his account for accommodation. The choice rests with the licensee. Credit may, but need not, be given for off-sales.

Employment of Young Persons

No person under 18 may be employed in a bar of licensed premises during permitted hours. Such a person would not be deemed to be employed in a bar by reason only of the fact that in the course of his employment in some other part of the premises he enters a bar for the purpose of giving or receiving any message, or is passing to or from some other part of the premises. In this context, the term 'bar' has a special definition (see page 138). The employment of a lounge waiter under eighteen who collects drinks from a dispense is probably outside the scope of this rule, though his position is doubtful.

THE CONDUCT OF LICENSED PREMISES

Children in a Bar
The licensee must not allow a child under 14 to be in a bar during permitted hours, but this rule does not apply to his own child or the child of a resident (not an employee) or where the child is passing through the bar to some other part of the premises.

Police
A police constable may enter licensed premises at any time up to the end of the first half-hour after permitted hours for the purpose of preventing or detecting the commission of any offence under the Licensing Act. He may enter at any time outside these hours where he suspects, with reasonable cause, that such an offence is being or is about to be committed there. He is also entitled to enter (i) premises for which an occasional licence is in force during the hours specified in the licence and (ii) premises for which a special hours certificate is in force from 11 p.m. until thirty minutes after the end of permitted hours.

Failure to admit a constable might render the licensee liable to a penalty. He must not bribe or attempt to bribe a constable, neither may any constable be supplied with liquor or refreshment except on the authority of his superior. The licensee must not harbour or knowingly allow any constable on duty to remain on the premises except in the execution of the constable's duty.

Offences
A licensee is liable to penalties if he fails to keep strictly to the provisions of the law, and for some offences there are heavy fines with or without imprisonment, and possible forfeiture of the licence. Among the more serious offences are selling without a licence, offences connected with prostitution, drunkenness or misbehaviour of customers, conduct inconsistent with the maintenance of good order, selling outside permitted hours, sale to or employment of persons under 18.

Unlicensed Premises
The law does not prevent the consumption on unlicensed premises by guests of their own liquor, but the occupier of the premises must not sell liquor in any circumstances, e.g. from his

own stock. If a guest asks him to purchase liquor, he or a member of his staff may act as agent for the guest, obtaining in advance the cash with which to make the purchase; if liquor is purchased without prepayment, and the proprietor puts the cost on the guest's account he would, in effect, be making an illegal sale.

THE LICENSING SYSTEM—Scotland

The Licensing (Scotland) Act 1976 repealed the Acts of 1959 and 1962. The sale of alcoholic liquor (formerly called intoxicating or excisable liquor) is now under the control of licensing boards which replace licensing courts. These boards grant licences instead of the former certificates, which do not require confirmation by a higher authority.

Licensing Authorities

A separate board is appointed for each district or islands area, or part thereof, as determined by the local council, with not less than a quarter of the council's members (minimum three). No one connected with the liquor trade may serve on a licensing board.

Every licensing board must meet in January, March, June and October on a day fixed six weeks beforehand, and at such other times as necessary. A quorum is one-half (minimum three) and decisions may be made on the following matters:

(a) applications for licences, including provisional grants;
(b) applications for renewals where competent objections have been lodged;
(c) refusal to grant a renewal;
(d) permanent transfer;
(e) applications for regular extensions of permitted hours;
(f) decisions concerning restricted hours;
(g) suspension of a licence;
(h) a closure order.

A licensing board may delegate decisions on other matters to a committee of the board, one or more members, the clerk to the board or a person appointed to assist the clerk.

Local Veto
The local veto system has been abolished, but areas in which no-licence or limiting resolutions applied on 30th June 1977 are subject to transitional provisions for up to three years.

Types of Licence
A licensing board may grant the following types of licence, authorising the sales mentioned, subject to any conditions the board may impose in individual premises:

Public House—consumption on or off the premises;

Off-sale—consumption off the premises only;

Hotel—consumption on or off the premises;

Restricted Hotel—to residents and their friends *bona fide* entertained by them, and to non-residents as an ancillary to table meals taken on the premises. The premises must be structurally adapted and *bona fide* used for lunch or dinner or both, and not have a bar counter;

Restaurant—with meals either at a bar or at table;

Refreshment—for consumption on the premises, when food and non-alcoholic beverages are also on sale; no bar counter;

Entertainment—as an ancillary to public entertainment at a cinema, theatre, dance hall or proprietary club, subject to conditions determined by licensing board.

How to apply for a Licence
An applicant, or his agent, must complete and sign a form obtainable from the clerk and lodge it with him not later than five weeks before the first day of a meeting, together with a plan of the premises. For at least 21 days before the first day of the meeting, he must also display at the premises, at a height where it can conveniently be read by the public, a notice in the prescribed form specifying the type of licence applied for. An application made otherwise than by an individual natural person (e.g. a company) must name both the applicant and the employee responsible for the day-to-day running of the premises.

Not later than three weeks before the first day of the meeting, the clerk is required to publish in one or more newspapers circulating in the area a list of competent applications to be considered at that meeting.

Hearing of Application

A licensing board considers new applications after all other cases have been dealt with, and may take into account any competent objections. An objection regarded as competent is one made by the owner or occupier of property in the neighbourhood of the premises, a local community council, an organised church representing a significant body of local opinion, or the chief constable. An objection must be in writing, and given to the board and the applicant at least seven days before the meeting. The board may decide to consider an objection by the chief constable at shorter notice if satisfied with the reason for delay provided the applicant is notified before the meeting. Objections can only be made on the following grounds:

(a) the applicant or prospective manager is not suitable;

(b) the premises are not suitable or convenient;

(c) the use of the premises for the sale of alcoholic liquor is likely to cause undue public nuisance, or a threat to public order or safety;

(d) to grant the application would result in over-provision of facilities.

A licensing board may refuse to consider an application unless the applicant or his agent is present. Otherwise it can only refuse to grant a licence on the grounds mentioned above and, in connection with (a) may have regard to any conviction against the applicant, whether constituting a breach of the Act or any byelaw, which the board considers reflects on his fitness to hold a licence.

An applicant refused a licence may appeal to the sheriff, and a competent objector may appeal against a grant, including any conditions which may have been attached. Applicants and objectors may request written reasons for a decision within 48 hours of its being made.

Grant of a Licence

Except in the case of an off-sale licence, the grant is subject to the production by the applicant of certificates from the appropriate authorities as to the suitability of the premises in relation to planning, building control and food hygiene. Before making a grant the board is required to consult the fire authority.

When granting any type of licence, the board may specify the liquor which may be supplied as (a) all types, (b) wine, porter, ale, beer, cider and perry, or (c) porter, ale, beer, cider and perry.

A new licence comes into effect on being granted, except where objection was made at the hearing, when its effect dates from the time when an appeal may be made and it has elapsed, or where an appeal has been lodged and then abandoned or determined in the applicant's favour. It then continues in effect until the quarterly meeting three years after the grant or renewal.

Provisional Grant of New Licence

An application for a provisional grant by a person interested in premises about to be constructed or in course of construction for use as licensed premises is similar to that for a new licence. A provisional grant needs to be affirmed within twelve months before becoming effective when the board declares the grant final.

Renewal

An applicant for the renewal of a licence, or his agent, has to submit an application not later than five weeks before the first day of the appropriate meeting. Except in the case of an off-sale licence, the licensing board cannot entertain such an application unless there is produced a certificate from the district or islands council concerned stating that the premises comply with the requirements of the Food & Drugs Act relating to construction, layout, drainage, ventilation, lighting and water supply, or concerned with the provision of sanitary and washing facilities. Before granting a renewal the board must consult the fire authority.

Transfer

An applicant for the *permanent* transfer of a licence, or his agent, must complete the appropriate form and lodge it with the clerk not later than five weeks before the board meets, provided he is a tenant or occupant. Where an employee, in a jointly-held licence ceases to have day-to-day responsibility for the premises, the licence will cease to have effect unless the transfer to another employee is made within eight weeks.

A *temporary* transfer, requiring confirmation at the next meeting, may be granted where a licensee has died or become bankrupt, insolvent or incapable, to an applicant in possession of the premises; the application has to be made by an executor, trustee or other person acting on behalf of the licensee.

Occasional Licence

A licensing board may grant an occasional licence to the holder of a licence, other than a refreshment or entertainment licence, authorising him to sell during such hours and on such days as the board may determine, in the course of catering for an event outwith licensed premises. It may impose conditions, any breach of which would constitute an offence. Application has to be made in writing to the clerk with a copy to the chief constable.

THE CONDUCT OF LICENSED PREMISES—
Scotland

Permitted Hours
Except for off-sale premises, the *week-day* permitted hours are 11 a.m. to 2.30 p.m. and 5 to 11 p.m.

In off-sale premises, including the off-sale parts of hotels and public houses, the permitted hours are not earlier than 8 a.m. to not later than 10 p.m.

Supply may be made with a meal up to 4 p.m. and in the evening to 1 a.m. in approved premises, which are those structurally adapted and *bona fide* used for the purpose of habitually providing, for the accommodation of persons frequenting the premises, substantial refreshment to which the sale and supply of alcoholic liquor is ancillary, and which have been approved by the appropriate licensing board. Only these premises may, subject to 14 days' notice to the chief constable, put the extended hours into effect and exhibit the relevant notice.

On *Sundays,* the permitted hours in premises to which an hotel, restricted hotel, restaurant or entertainment licence applies are from 12.30 to 2.30 p.m. and 6.30 to 11 p.m. These hours also apply to premises with a public house or refreshment licence where an application for Sunday opening has been granted. Such an application can be made after giving the clerk not less than five weeks' notice before a meeting of the board and displaying an appropriate notice on the premises. The board has discretion to refuse, when the applicant may appeal to the sheriff.

Supply may be made with a meal in approved premises from 12.30 to 4 p.m. and from 5 p.m. to 1 a.m. on giving 14 days' notice to the chief constable. A restaurant in premises with a

THE CONDUCT OF LICENSED PREMISES

public house licence but without Sunday opening may serve alcoholic liquor with a meal, subject to the bar being closed.

Consumption after the end of any session of permitted hours may take place during the first 15 minutes, or thirty minutes with a meal.

Extension of Permitted Hours

A board may grant an application for a *regular* extension of permitted hours if it considers it desirable to do so in the public interest, and may impose conditions after taking account of any competent objections.

A board may grant an application for an *occasional* extension on an occasion it considers appropriate, not exceeding one month.

Copy of an application for an extension must be sent to the chief constable.

Restriction Order

A board has power to make an order restricting evening permitted hours to 10 p.m. if satisfied that the sale of alcoholic liquor is the cause of undue public nuisance or constitutes a threat to public order or safety.

Regulations and Bye-Laws

A licensing board may make regulations concerning applications for licences, including occasional licences, extension of permitted hours, provisions to assist the board in determining the fitness of applicants to hold a licence, the procedure for transferring licences and other matters.

It may also make bye-laws, which require confirmation by the Secretary of State, for any of the following:

1. closing licensed premises wholly or partially on New Year's Day and on not more than four others in any one year for special reasons;

2. prohibiting the holders of licences from residing in their licensed premises or for requiring dwelling-houses of licensees to be separate from their licensed premises;

3. requiring sales of wines and spirits in off-sale premises to be in corked, stoppered or sealed vessels, except where no groceries are kept or sold and where a *bona fide* wholesale business is carried on;

4. requiring every holder of an hotel or public house licence to keep a fresh and sufficient supply of drinking water and such eatables as may be specified, and to display, offer and supply as required by the bye-law.

Breach of a bye-law constitutes an offence.

Provision is also made enabling a board to suspend a licence on receipt of a complaint where the board is satisfied that it is in the public interest to do so.

SALE OF LIQUOR

Part VI, comprising 35 sections, and Schedule 5 of the Act are concerned with offences both by licensees and customers. A licensee has general responsibility for the proper conduct of his premises, including vicarious responsibility for the actions of his employees and agents. Where an offence is committed without his knowledge, he might escape a penalty if he can prove that he had exercised all due diligence to prevent it. In the case of a company, proceedings may be taken against the company itself and any director or official responsible. Penalties range from £10 to £400 and may also involve disqualification of the licensee and/or the premises for up to five years.

The following are the principal matters affecting licensees:

1. The sale of liquor in a bar to a person under 18 is prohibited and it is an offence for any person knowingly to act as agent for a person under 18 or attempt to purchase liquor for his consumption. (The wording of this provision differs from the English one as the word 'knowingly' is not applicable to the licensee).

A person who has attained the age of 16 may purchase or be served with beer, wine, made wine, porter, cider or perry for consumption at a meal in a place set apart for meals not being a bar or in a bar.

The licensee or his employee must not deliver to a person under 18 any liquor for consumption off the premises except

THE CONDUCT OF LICENSED PREMISES

at his residence or working-place. No one may knowingly send a person under 18 to obtain liquor from licensed premises, but a member of the licensee's family or staff under 18 may act as messenger to deliver liquor.

2. Children under 14 are not allowed in a bar during permitted hours; exceptions are a child of the licensee or of a resident other than an employee. If accompanied by a person of 21 or over, a child may be allowed in premises with a refreshment licence up to 8 p.m.

3. A person under 18 must not be employed in a bar during permitted hours; a person under 18 must not be employed to serve liquor in premises with a refreshment licence.

4. Drunken persons must not be supplied with alcoholic liquor, and the police may arrest drunken persons who refuse to leave licensed premises when requested to do so.

5. A licensee must not permit thieves, prostitutes or stolen goods on his premises.

6. A police constable may enter and inspect licensed premises, other than off-sale premises, at any time. He may enter off-sale premises and any temperance hotel, restaurant or other place where food or drink is sold for consumption on the premises if he has reasonable grounds for believing that alcoholic liquor is being trafficked unlawfully and he has written authority to do so.

7. A licensee must not knowingly allow any constable to remain on the premises beyond the time necessary for the execution of his duty nor knowingly supply him with liquor or refreshment while on duty except with the authority of a superior officer.

8. The sale of liquor on credit is prohibited, except that supply with a meal may be paid for with the meal, and supply to a resident may be paid for with his accommodation.

Credit tokens may be accepted, but not in a public bar, in premises with an hotel, restricted hotel, restaurant or entertainment licence.

9. In premises with a restricted hotel, restaurant, refreshment or entertainment licence, the licensee must have strict

regard to the limitations which the licence imposes on the sale of liquor.

In the application of weights and measures legislation to Scotland the provisions shown as item 5 on page 99 are modified to the extent that measures for beer and cider apply to quantities of one pint or more.

REGISTERED CLUBS

Where liquor is proposed to be supplied in a club, the club must be either registered or licensed. Registration of a club allows its members to consume liquor in private subject to certain conditions, which, while broadly similar, are not the same in Scotland as in England and Wales.

England and Wales

Qualifications for registration

The following are the principal requirements;

(a) the club must be established and conducted in good faith;

(b) there must be at least 25 members;

(c) the rules must provide that applicants for membership cannot be admitted to the privileges of membership without an interval of two days between application and admission;

(d) liquor must be supplied only by and on behalf of the club;

(e) purchase and sale of liquor must be under the control of members or a committee of them.

In addition, there must be no arrangement for any person to receive at the expense of the club any payment by way of commission on purchases of liquor, and no person may directly or indirectly derive any pecuniary benefit from the supply of liquor to members or guests.

In determining whether a club is established and conducted in good faith, a magistrates' court may have regard to:

(a) any arrangement restricting the club's freedom to purchase;

(b) any arrangement whereby any gain from carrying on the club is not applied for the benefit of the club as a whole or for charitable, benevolent or political purposes;

(c) the giving of proper information to members about the finances of the club;

(d) the nature of the premises occupied by the club.

Provisions as to club rules form the 7th schedule to the 1964 Act.

Application for registration certificate

An application must specify the name, objects and address of the club, and state that a list of the names and addresses of members is kept there. Sufficient information must be given to show that the club is qualified to receive a registration certificate, a copy of the rules must be supplied, with a list showing the names and addresses of members of a general management committee responsible for the purchase and supply of liquor. Particulars must also be given as to the interest of the club in its premises and any other premises it may use, with any liability charged on it. An application must be signed by the chairman or secretary of the club.

Procedure for registration

Application is made to a magistrates' court, through the clerk to the justices, who sends copies to the chief officer of police and the clerk to the local authority. At the same time the club must display a notice on or near the premises for seven days beginning with the date of application and advertise the fact on at least one of those days in a local newspaper.

Before first registration, the premises may be inspected by a police constable, an officer of the local authority and an officer of the fire authority..

An objection to the issue or renewal of a certificate may be made, within 21 days after the date of application, to the clerk to the justices who will send a copy to the applicant. The ground of objection must be specified.

A magistrates' court may refuse an application on the ground that the qualifying conditions have not been met. There is an appeal to a crown court against a refusal or any condition imposed.

A registration certificate is valid for 12 months and may be renewed or surrendered. Renewal will be for one year in the first instance but a subsequent renewal may be for any period up to ten years.

Conduct of clubs

Clubs must keep to the permitted hours specified in the rules, which need not be the same as those applicable to licensed premises in the district, but must not exceed them either in number of the period covered. There must be a break of at least two hours in the afternoon, and on Sundays, Christmas Day and Good Friday it must include the period 3 to 5 p.m., followed by not more than 3½ permitted hours of supply. In Wales, registered clubs are not affected by any decision to close licensed premises on Sundays.

The rules applicable to licensed premises concerning supply of liquor with meals, to residents, and during extended hours where the requisite authority has been obtained, apply equally to clubs.

Scotland

The sheriff clerk acts as registrar, and the chairman, secretary or solicitor of a club is required to lodge an application with him for a certificate stating the name, objects and address of the club, and enclosing:

(a) two copies of the rules;

(b) a list containing the name and address of every official and committee of management member;

(c) a statement in the appropriate form that the club is to be conducted as a *bona fide* club and not mainly for the supply of alcoholic liquor; the form has to be counter-signed by two members of the licensing board and also by the owner of the premises if not the club.

The applicant must advertise the lodging of the application and post a notice on the premises for the following 21 days. The sheriff notifies the chief constable, the local council and the fire authority. Objections may be made by the same persons as could object to a licence, with a copy to the club secretary.

Twenty grounds are specified in the Act as competent for objections, and the sheriff's decision in dealing with an application is final.

The club rules must include provision for management to be by an elected committee, no member of which may have an interest in the sale of alcoholic liquor or the profits arising from sales; no sale or supply to any person under 18; no person under 18 to be admitted a member unless the club is primarily concerned with athletics or is for students of a recognised educational establishment. Provision may be made for the interchange of membership facilities between visiting clubs.

A registration certificate is valid for three years.

Permitted hours in clubs are the same as for licensed premises, but athletic clubs may apply to the sheriff for alternative hours in the winter.

In both countries

No one under 14 is allowed in a club bar and no one under 18 may serve alcoholic liquor.

The police may enter a club only by warrant.

VARIOUS LICENCES

Billiards
A licence for the playing of billiards and similar games is not required for fully-licensed premises, neither is one necessary for an hotel or guest house if available only to residents and their private friends. Otherwise, a table accessible to the general public must be licensed under the Gaming Act.

Music and Dancing
In premises licensed for the sale of liquor in England and Wales a music and dancing licence is not required where entertainment is provided by radio or television, or music and singing by not more than two performers in person.

Apart from this, the law concerning *public* music and dancing in premises forming part of an hotel or restaurant is not uniform throughout the country.

Originally, the Disorderly Houses Act 1751 provided that no house, room, garden or other place could be kept for public dancing, music or other public entertainment of the like kind without a licence from the county council. In principle, this is the position today only:

1. where a local Act of Parliament applies;
2. where Part IV of the Public Health Acts (Amendment) Act of 1890 applies, by choice of the local authority.

A licence, where required, may authorise *public* entertainment in premises regularly used for the purpose; it may also permit *private* entertainment in premises where it is promoted for private gain. Local bye-laws should be consulted.

The significance of a music and dancing licence is that an application for a special hours certificate cannot be made without one.

Performing Right

Under the Copyright Act 1956, any unauthorised performance *in public* of copyright music is an infringement of that copyright, which normally belongs to the composer and his assigns up to fifty years after his death. There is a performance in public when members of the public can hear it in a place where they have paid to be, such as an hotel (except in a bedroom), restaurant, theatre or public-house. Persons attending a function for which they have purchased a ticket are also members of the public for this purpose.

It makes no difference how the music is performed, whether by artistes in person or by radio, television or gramophone.

The Performing Right Society acts on behalf of the majority of owners of copyright in music and issues licences on their behalf to hotels, restaurants and other premises concerned.

The manufacturer of a record or tape has a separate copyright in the recording, irrespective of the music or other material recorded on it, but the Act provides that there is no infringement where the recording can be heard in public at any premises where persons reside or sleep, as part of the amenities provided exclusively or mainly for residents. This provision does not affect any copyright in music on a record in which the Performing Right Society has an interest. If the music and the record are both subject to copyright, two licences are required. The copyright in most records is held by Phonographic Performance Ltd.

Late Night Refreshment House

A licence is required in England and Wales for premises kept open at any time between 10 p.m. and 5 a.m. for public refreshment, resort or entertainment if no licence for the sale of liquor is held.

Application is made to the local authority, and a grant is for one year, renewable on 1st April. Conditions may be imposed as to opening after 11 p.m. if the authority is satisfied that it is desirable in order to avoid unreasonable disturbance of local residents. A tariff of charges must be exhibited.

The police may visit a refreshment house and rules as to the conduct of the premises are similar to those applicable to licensed premises. There are penalties for keeping a refreshment house without a licence; the proprietor if not resident must notify his address, and a person using the premises while drunk is liable to a fine.

In Scotland, a person who keeps a place of public refreshment which is open at any time between 8 p.m. and 5 a.m. or at any time on Sunday must register with the local authority. A place of public refreshment includes 'any building or part of a building or other place of public resort for the sale for consumption therein of provisions or refreshments of any kind (including confectionery, ice cream, fruit and aerated waters) not licensed for the sale of alcoholic liquor.

Tobacco

An excise licence is not required for the retail sale of tobacco. At premises licensed for the sale of liquor, tobacco may be sold during permitted hours, otherwise the hours of sale will depend on the Shops Act. There are penalties for sale to persons under sixteen and restrictions may be placed on the location of automatic machines if extensively used by persons under sixteen.

Betting and Gaming

Licensed premises must not be used for *betting* or for receiving bets. No offence is, however, committed where all the persons concerned in betting transactions live or work on the premises, or have a bookmaker's permit.

Gaming—which means the playing of a game of chance for winnings in money or money's worth—is lawful on both licensed and unlicensed premises, in certain circumstances and subject to certain safeguards. It is convenient to explain the situation as it applies (a) in places accessible to the public generally, and (b) in private rooms available only to residents or members of a club.

In *public places,* all games of pure skill (e.g. billiards, darts) are permitted without restriction. Dominoes and cribbage are also permitted, but in licensed premises the justices (in Scotland, the licensing board) may restrict play if high stakes are regularly involved or the playing of such games is the main inducement for persons to resort to the premises. Other games (e.g. bridge) may be played at an entertainment promoted to raise money for charitable purposes, so long as the playing does not result in private gain.

Gaming machines—amusements with prizes—may be installed provided the occupier has a permit from the licensing justices (licensing board) or the local authority, if unlicensed, all these authorities having power to limit the number of machines. Stakes must not exceed 5p per game, with a maximum cash prize of 15p or tokens worth 40p. Machines must be bought outright or rented for a fixed sum, as profit-sharing of takings is not permitted. Excise duty and VAT are payable.

In *private rooms* all games are permitted so long as conditions ensure fair play. No one under 18 may take part unless accompanied by a parent or guardian who agrees to his doing so. The only payment allowed is stake money, which must all be distributed as winnings to a player.

Not more than two gaming machines are allowed; stakes must not exceed 5p and all stakes must be paid out as winnings or for purposes other than private gain. A permit is required and excise duty and VAT are payable.

OBLIGATIONS OF THE PROPRIETOR

A number of subjects may conveniently be considered in this chapter, which is intended to cover items incidental to the proprietor's main functions. The authors have decided to omit references to taxation, including value added tax, and national insurance, as they consider these are more appropriate to a book on accounting and leaflets are available explaining them in detail. They also assume the reader will consult a solicitor when buying a business and a planning officer when contemplating an extension, making comments only on those aspects of special concern in this industry.

Purchase and Sale of a business

The contract covering the transfer of a business, as distinct from the premises in which it is conducted, is of special importance to the purchaser, and he should watch the following points:

1. The items he is buying, e.g.

    (a) Furniture and equipment should be detailed in an inventory, and an undertaking given by the vendor that every item is his own property, any on hire being shown separately.

    (b) Goodwill, if included in the sale, either specifically or by implication, should be supported by some proof of the volume of business done. The purchaser would expect to have the benefit of current and future bookings as from an agreed date, and he might consider whether to ask for an undertaking by the vendor not to conduct a similar business in the vicinity. An agreement in restraint of trade would be void unless: (i) it is reasonably necessary to protect the purchaser, (ii) it is not unreasonable to the vendor, and (iii) it is not injurious to the public.

(c) Transfer of a lease will involve obtaining the consent of the landlord, with the new tenant taking over the rights and obligations of the former tenant.

2. If the premises are licensed for the sale of liquor, the purchaser will have to apply for a transfer, and an agreement may contain a clause to the effect that the vendor will facilitate transfer to the new owner.

3. Standing and other charges will have to be apportioned as between vendor and purchaser for the current period.

4. Outstanding contracts. Any obligations of the vendor which may devolve on the purchaser should be disclosed, e.g. advertising, goods on hire.

5. Staff. If the purchaser intends to employ the vendor's staff, agreement is needed on liability for holiday pay; an employee not re-engaged may have a claim for redundancy pay from the vendor.

The one-man business

A sole trader, in effect, ventures all his resources and takes full responsibility for the conduct of his business. If there are profits, they belong to him, and if there are losses he must shoulder them even to the extent of realising, if need be, all his assets and, in default may be made bankrupt.

So long as he conducts the business in his own name, no formalities are involved, but if he does not do so it would be necessary to register the business name with the Registrar of Business Names; failure to register could mean inability to enforce a contract.

Partnership

Two or more persons carrying on business together as partners are in a similar position to sole traders inasmuch as they venture all their resources in the enterprise. In the first instance they will contribute an agreed amount of capital, and decide in what proportions profits will be shared and losses borne. If liabilities should at any time exceed available assets, further contributions

OBLIGATIONS OF THE PROPRIETOR

from the partners may be required to preserve solvency. There are many husband and wife partnerships in this industry where a formal agreement may not be necessary, but otherwise a deed would be useful to establish business relationships.

There is one exception to the unlimited liability of partners and this arises where a limited partner, sometimes called a sleeping partner, is admitted. He will contribute capital but take no part in the conduct of the business.

Company

There are advantages in organising a business as a company, and this form of ownership is now common for hotels and other catering concerns, from the small private enterprise to the mammoth public company receiving its main financial support from the public at large. A business may start as a company, even on a small scale. Established businesses starting as sole traders or partnerships may later be converted into companies. This chapter will explain, in outline, the law relating to companies, showing the procedure for formation and the general lines of administration.

The principal advantages of incorporation are:

1. The liability of the members of the company (i.e. the shareholders) is limited to the amount, if any, payable in respect of their shares. This is one of the principal distinctions from a partnership, and means that once shares are fully paid no further demand can be made on the shareholders whatever the financial state of the company.

2. By allotting shares to correspond to the interests of those engaged in the business, either actively or otherwise, it is possible to provide in a simple way for profits to be shared by the payment of dividends, for the transfer of such interests when a shareholder wishes to dispose of them without affecting the finances of the company, and for the division of the assets in the event of sale or winding-up.

3. The death, bankruptcy or incapacity of any director or other shareholder does not affect the continuance of the business or impose any liability on the other members.

4. Facilities are more readily available for borrowing money or raising additional capital.

5. The number of persons who may contribute to the capital of a company is unlimited, except so far as private companies are concerned.

A company, unlike a partnership, is a legal entity; that is, it is regarded in law as an individual person and as having the same capacity to do business as an ordinary citizen. This separate legal existence is the fundamental feature of the company which, again unlike a partnership, goes on indefinitely in spite of changes in the shareholders or directors, and only comes to an end when 'wound up' or 'liquidated'. A company can make contracts, employ staff, have a bank account, and sue and be sued in its own name. Its functions are carried out by directors, but the death or retirement of a director makes no difference to the existence of the company in the eyes of the law.

Incorporation

Before a company can come into existence, its promoters or founders must apply to the Registrar of Joint Stock Companies at the appropriate office in England or Scotland, for incorporation of the company and for this purpose must submit the following documents:

1. Memorandum of Association;
2. Articles of Association;
3. Statement of Nominal Capital;
4. Declaration of compliance with Companies Acts.

The *Memorandum* is, in effect, a request for incorporation, signed by the subscribers, giving the following information:

(a) The *Name* of the company. A name must be chosen which does not so closely resemble another already on the register as to be likely to deceive. The name of a trading company must end with the word 'Limited'. If the name is similar to another on the register or the department concerned considers it to be undesirable, the Registrar may decline to register it.

OBLIGATIONS OF THE PROPRIETOR

(b) The *Registered Office* of the company. At this stage it is necessary merely to state whether the office will be in England, Wales or Scotland.

(c) The *Objects* of the company. As this clause determines the powers of the company, the objects are usually set out in considerable detail so as to include every possible activity in which the company might be engaged. In the Courts, a Memorandum would be strictly construed, though it has been held that a company may do any acts which are considered 'fairly incidental' to the objects listed in the Memorandum. If necessary, the Memorandum can be altered by special resolution of the shareholders.

(d) A statement that the *liability of the members* is limited.

(e) The amount of the *Share Capital,* the number of shares into which it is divided and the nominal amount of each. The amount of capital may be increased by the company in general meeting by passing a resolution in accordance with the Articles; a reduction of capital must have the consent of the appropriate court.

The Memorandum must be signed by not less than 7 persons in the case of a public company and not less than 2 in the case of a private company.

The *Articles of Association* are the internal rules of the company, the regulations for management, covering such matters as appointment, powers and duties of directors, allotment and transfer of shares, procedure at meetings, voting rights and so on.

All the documents mentioned have to be stamped at current rates. When they have been accepted by the Registrar, he issues a Certificate of Incorporation, and from its date the company begins its separate existence as a legal 'person'.

Public and Private Companies

Companies may be public or private. The main distinction between them is that public companies may invite the public to subscribe capital whereas a private company is prohibited from so doing.

While a public company must fulfil certain statutory requirements before commencing business, a private company may do so immediately on incorporation. The administrative requirements of a private company are also simpler as it can consist of two or more persons up to a maximum of fifty, excluding past and present employees; it need have only one director, though he may not act as secretary as well. There must be a registered office; an auditor must be appointed who cannot be a director or officer of the company. An annual report has to be filed with accounts containing certain specified information. Details are best studied in a book on Company Law.

Planning

A series of Town and Country Planning Acts have given the State control over the development of land, much of which is now under the administration of local authorities. The principal matters of concern to the hotel and catering industry may be summarised as follows: new buildings require planning permission; some existing buildings may be converted to other uses without permission, while other changes require permission; extensions or alterations may or may not require permission. While it is advisable to consult the local planning officer for detailed information, the general principles are:

1. A Use Classes Order provides that the conversion of a shop to a restaurant, a fried fish shop or a tripe shop requires planning permission; changes involving an hotel, on-licensed premises or a service garage also require permission; but no permission is required to change most other kinds of shop to other shop uses.

2. The conversion of a private house to a business, e.g. a guest house, requires permission.

3. Building alterations which do not materially affect the external appearance do not require permission and certain extensions of a limited nature are also permissible.

Advertisements

Advertisements displayed on business premises which relate to the business there carried on do not require express consent under the Advertisement Control Regulations, unless *illuminated*. In an area of special control, such as a National Park, there would be a limitation on size. An advertisement in the form of a flag, which is attached to a single flagstaff fixed in an upright position on the roof of a building, may be displayed without special consent provided it bears only the name or device of the occupier. No letter or figure in any of these advertisements may exceed 30 in. (76 cm.) in height, or in an area of special control 12 in. (30 cm.).

All other advertisements require express consent, application for which has to be made on a form issued by the planning authority. There is an appeal to the appropriate Minister against refusal.

The Shops Act
Certain shops may be open on Sundays in England and Wales, and the commodities which may be sold on Sundays include:

(a) Intoxicating liquor (subject to permitted hours);

(b) Meals or refreshments, whether or not for consumption on the premises, but not including the sale of fried fish and chips at a fried fish shop;

(c) Newly-cooked provisions and cooked or partly-cooked tripe;

(d) Table waters, sweets, chocolates, sugar confectionery and ice cream, including wafers and edible containers;

(e) Fodder for horses, mules, ponies and donkeys at any hotel or inn;

(f) Flowers, fresh fruit, fresh vegetables, milk;

(g) Tobacco.

A local authority may make a partial exemption order permitting shops to open on Sunday up to 10 a.m. for the sale of bread, fish or groceries.

At holiday resorts, the local authority may permit certain shops to be open on not more than 18 Sundays for the sale of specified articles, including photographic requisites, toys, souvenirs, books, stationery, bathing costumes and fishing tackle.

On Sundays, hairdressers may attend customers at an hotel, but must not carry on business or employ assistants in their own premises.

These provisions concerning Sunday opening of shops are, generally, not applicable in Scotland, but shops may open provided local bye-laws permit.

Powers of Local Authorities

Under several Public Health Acts, local authorities may take action to protect the public in certain buildings and to require means of escape from fire to be provided; these requirements are usually set out in bye-laws.

Before any building can be constructed or used, at which a number of persons are likely to resort at one time, plans must be deposited with the local authority showing entrances, exits, passages and gangways to be provided. The person having control of such a building must observe the authority's directions, which are intended to ensure adequate measures being maintained to enable the public to leave the building quickly in the event of emergency. These provisions apply to any building used as a place of public resort. In conjunction with the Fire Precautions Act, almost all premises in the hotel and catering industry are now subject to controls of this nature (see also page 34).

Sanitary conveniences

A local authority may require the owner or occupier of an inn, public house, refreshment house or place of public entertainment to provide and maintain a reasonable number of sanitary conveniences. There are penalties for failure to comply.

Water

A local authority or statutory water undertaking supplying water for domestic purposes may apply to the Minister concerned to fix a maximum charge per 1,000 gallons of water by meter, subject to the right of the authority to make a minimum charge. The authority may require all water supplied to a club, hostel, place of public entertainment, hotel, licensed premises, or a boarding-house (capable of accommodating 12 or more persons) to be taken by meter.

Collection of Refuse

Under the Control of Pollution Act, refuse from hotels and restaurants is classified as 'commercial waste', which local collection authorities are obliged to collect on request, but for which they are entitled to make a reasonable charge. They may provide receptacles for the purpose. In certain small premises, refuse may continue to be regarded as 'household waste' and collected without separate charge.

LANDLORD AND TENANT (England and Wales)

Security of tenure for tenants of business premises is now provided in the Law of Property Act 1969. A tenant who qualifies for protection may be an individual or a company, with a lease or written tenancy agreement or an oral agreement. The tenancy may be for a specific term, or on a weekly, monthly, quarterly or yearly basis. The tenant is protected if he conducts a business, trade or profession on the premises, as for example, an hotel, a restaurant, guest house or club. But he is not protected if he is the tenant of on-licensed premises where the main business is the sale of liquor, e.g. a public house, though an hotel or restaurant is likely to be protected.

Protected tenants can, if they wish, stay in the premises after the tenancy comes to an end, on the same terms, unless the landlord terminates the tenancy either by offering a new tenancy at agreed terms, or by giving notice. In the latter case, if the landlord is unwilling to grant a new tenancy, or if terms for a new tenancy cannot be agreed, the tenant may apply to the county court for a new tenancy. The court will grant a new tenancy unless the landlord can establish his case for possession on one of the following grounds:

1. The tenant has failed to comply with the terms of his tenancy, or is otherwise unsatisfactory;

2. The landlord offers suitable alternative accommodation;

3. Where the tenant occupies only part of the premises, and the landlord can let or sell and would suffer substantial loss if he cannot obtain possession of the tenant's part;

4. The landlord requires the premises for demolition or reconstruction;

5. The landlord intends to occupy the premises himself, either for business or residence, but he cannot claim possession where he bought the property less than five years before the end of the tenancy.

Where a tenant is refused a new tenancy by reason of 3, 4 or 5 above, compensation is payable by the landlord to the tenant when he leaves, the amount being equivalent to the rateable value if he has carried on business for less than 14 years, and double the rateable value if he has done so for 14 years or more.

Compensation for improvement

In order to qualify for compensation for improvement, the tenant must have obtained the approval of the landlord for the improvement to be made. This he must do by serving a notice on him of his intention, together with a plan and specification showing the proposed improvement and the part of the premises affected.

On receipt of such notice, the landlord may object, in which event the tenant may apply to the county court for a certificate that the improvement is a proper one, and the tenant can proceed with the work if the certificate is given. If the landlord does not serve notice of objection to the proposal within three months the tenant will be entitled to execute the work in accordance with the plan and specification.

The court may grant a certificate only if it is satisfied that the improvement is of such a nature as to be calculated to add to the letting value of the holding at the termination of the tenancy, and is reasonable and suitable to the character thereof, and will not diminish the value of any other property belonging to the same landlord.

Notice of intention to claim compensation for improvement must be given by the tenant to the landlord in the manner prescribed by county court rules:

(a) Within one month of service of Notice to Quit; or

(b) Not more than 36 months nor less than 12 months before the expiration of the lease.

Where the tenant continues in occupation, improvements made by the tenant are to be disregarded when fixing the rent.

These provisions do not apply in Scotland.

BUSINESS INSURANCE

The operation of a business in the hotel and catering industry involves risks to property, equipment and goods, and also to people, the consequences of which can and should be covered by insurance. A company or person who stands to lose financially can contract with an insurer (Lloyds or an insurance company) whereby, in return for a premium and subject to stated conditions, the insured can be indemnified against such loss. Each kind of risk may be the subject of a separate policy, or a number of risks can be combined into one policy (sometimes called a comprehensive policy) designed for a particular trade.

An hotel comprehensive policy, for example, would normally cover the following groups of risk: fire, special perils (storm and tempest, earthquake, riot and civil commotion, malicious damage, impact by vehicles or aircraft), burglary, accidents to staff (employer's liability), public liability (guests, customers and others), safety of cash (cash in transit). Such a combined policy may allow for other risks to be covered or these may be the subject of separate policies: examples are plate and other glass, boilers, lifts, other machinery, vehicles, neon signs. Fidelity guarantee insurance may also be arranged in respect of staff handling cash or other valuables.

A fire policy would apply to buildings and their contents, whether belonging to the insured or his guests, and might provide compensation in the form of money or reinstatement.

The risk that continuance of a business may be jeopardised either partly or wholly by a fire or other damage can be covered by a consequential loss policy or provision in a comprehensive policy, and this is intended to indemnify the insured against loss of profit, the payment of standing charges (rent, rates, etc.) and additional expense incurred in moving to and occupation of temporary premises. A policy can also be extended to cover loss suffered by the insured from other unforeseen causes, such as a murder or suicide, food poisoning, or infectious disease.

An employer's obligation to insure in respect of accidents to staff is explained on page 42.

Liability to members of the public may arise under a number of headings:

(a) An hotel proprietor has special liability in respect of loss or damage to guests' property;

(b) A private hotel proprietor has liability for negligence only;

(c) An hotel proprietor may have responsibility as bailee for items outside his legal liability under the 1956 Act, e.g. cars and animals. A person not an hotel proprietor may accept articles for safe custody, such as hats and coats. It is not unusual for such liabilities to be limited by a disclaimer notice, but this may be subject to the Unfair Contract Terms Act (see page 19);

(d) Injury caused by defective premises (insufficient lighting, slippery floors, projecting nails, etc.). Cover should extend to all persons lawfully on the premises, e.g. postmen, decorators, etc.

(e) Food poisoning and other injury arising from the service of food and drink.

Safety of cash is normally covered only when in transit to and from a bank; loss of cash from other causes is insurable only when in a locked safe and burglary or housebreaking is involved.

In practice, insurers offer standard policies and assess premiums on a recognised basis; within limitations, alterations and additions may be made to suit individual requirements. Each policy or section of a combined policy must state the maximum liability of the insurer or express in money terms the basis of the contract. As a contract of insurance depends on the utmost good faith of the parties, an insured who did not disclose all material information might find that, under its terms, the insurer could avoid liability, either wholly or in part. Underinsurance of a risk as, for example, insuring a building for much less than its real value in a fire policy, would lead to a claim being subject to average. This means that the insurer's liability would not exceed the proportion which the insured value bears to the true value.

PURCHASES

The rights of a purchaser against a supplier may be the subject of an agreement or may be implied from the nature of the contract. Implied conditions include the following:

1. In a sale by description the goods must be adequate for the purpose for which such goods would normally be used;

2. The goods must be fit for a particular purpose where such a condition has become accepted by the usage of trade;

3. Where goods are sold by sample, the bulk must correspond with the sample in quality;

4. The seller has the right to sell the goods.

A condition in a contract is so essential to its nature that a breach of it gives the party not in default the right to treat the contract as at an end.

These provisions have been reinforced by subsequent legislation intended to protect the interest of the consumer. No longer can the supplier of goods or the provider of services avoid liability for negligence, and contract terms purporting to limit his responsibilities will either be void or subject to the test of reasonableness. The most recent statute is the Unfair Contract Terms Act 1977.

Hire Purchase

Where articles are obtained on hire purchase, the provisions of the Hire Purchase Act 1965 may apply. This Act is concerned with hire purchase and credit sale agreements where the total sum payable (excluding any penalty, compensation or damages) does not exceed £2,000. The main points are:

1. Before the agreement is entered into the owner must state the cash price in writing.

2. A memorandum must be signed by the hirer stating:

    (a) the hire purchase price;

    (b) the cash price;

    (c) dates and amounts of instalments;

    (d) a list of the items involved;

    (e) a notice in the terms prescribed setting out the hirer's rights under the contract including, where applicable, the hirer's option to cancel within four days.

3. If the requirements in 2 above are not complied with, the contract cannot be enforced, neither can the goods be recovered. The court has power, however, to dispense with any of the requirements other than the making of the memorandum if it is satisfied that the hirer has not been prejudiced.

4. Where one-third of the hire purchase price has been paid or tendered, the owner cannot enforce any right except by process of law.

A credit sale is one where ownership of the goods passes immediately and the price is payable by five or more instalments.

Similar legislation applies in Scotland.

Laundry

The form of contract between hotels and laundries may be the subject of agreement or standard conditions applicable in the case of domestic customers may apply.

Some of the more usual provisions are as follow:

1. No article exposed to infection may be sent to a laundry; to do so would be an offence under Public Health Acts.

2. The laundry has a general lien on articles sent by a customer for all charges due.

3. Compensation for loss or damage of articles while in the possession of the laundry as the result of negligence of the laundry's employees may be subject to a maximum amount related to charge for washing.

4. A laundry may refuse responsibility for any of the following:

(a) Damage arising from defective manufacture, deterioration from wear, stains or other defects;

(b) Damage arising from fugitive colours, shrinkage or distortion, unsuitable or faulty material, or incorrectly described articles;

(c) Damage to curtains or blinds;

(d) Loss of any article not indelibly and distinctly marked with the customer's name in full;

(e) Loss of any article not plainly described in the

OBLIGATIONS OF THE PROPRIETOR

book or list bearing the customer's name and address sent to the laundry with the article;

(f) Loss of any money, jewellery or valuables included with any article sent to the laundry;

(g) Absence of proof that the article was duly received by the laundry.

Where an hotel installs laundry machinery on its own premises and employs staff solely or mainly for this purpose, it is likely that the Factories Act will apply, in which case certain obligations under that Act must be observed. The local factory inspector should be consulted. The wages of staff employed will be governed by orders made by the Laundry Wages Council.

GLOSSARY OF LEGAL TERMS

Alcoholic liquor: Spirits, wine, porter, ale, beer, cider, perry, and made-wine, of over 1,016 degrees original gravity and over two degrees of proof; this term is used in the Licensing (Scotland) Act 1976 to replace 'exciseable' or 'intoxicating' liquor.

Bailee: A person to whom goods are delivered by another person (called the Bailor) who has no intention of transferring the property in such goods and who does so on the condition that they are re-delivered to the bailor or according to his instructions as soon as the purpose for which they have been bailed has been fulfilled. Example—a cloakroom attendant normally an employee or agent of the management.

Bar: Any open drinking bar or any part of premises exclusively or mainly used for the sale and consumption of intoxicating (alcoholic) liquor. This definition does not include a bar when it is set apart for the service of table meals and the sale of liquor is limited to persons having table meals there as an ancillary thereto.

Beer: Includes ale, porter, stout, and any other description of beer which is made or sold as a description of beer or as a substitute for beer, and which on analysis of a sample thereof at any time is found to contain more than 2 per cent of proof spirit.

Child: A person under 14 years of age.

Clerk to the Justices: The title of the official, in England and Wales, who attends to the administrative work of the Justices.

Contract: An agreement, either verbal or in writing, between two or more persons, which is enforceable at law.

County court: In England and Wales, a court in certain urban areas, with jurisdiction in civil cases, e.g. breach of contract, debt, bankruptcy.

Court of session: In Scotland, the superior civil court which may be a court of first instance or an appeal court.

Court of summary jurisdiction: see petty sessional court.

Crown courts: In England and Wales, the courts with jurisdiction in more serious criminal cases, which may consider appeals from decisions of licensing justices.

Deed: A written instrument which has been signed, sealed and delivered by the person or persons who are party to it. Certain contracts are required by law to be by deed, e.g. legal mortgages.

Fully-licensed premises: Premises at which the sale of spirits, wine, beer, and cider is authorised for consumption on and off the premises.

Holding-over: A tenant holds over who remains in possession of property after the expiration of his lease.

Hotel: In Scotland, a house in towns and suburbs containing at least four apartments set apart exclusively for the sleeping accommodation of travellers; or, in rural districts with not more than 1,000 population, a house containing at least two such apartments.

Imperial measure: A measure of capacity laid down by the Weights and Measures Acts, as distinct from metric measures.

Intoxicating liquor: In England and Wales, spirits, wine, beer, cider, British wine, and any other fermented, distilled or spirituous liquor. In Scotland, alcoholic liquor.

Libel: Defamatory matter in writing or other permanent form which tends to expose a person to hatred, ridicule, or contempt, or causes him to be shunned, or injures him in his office.

Lien: The right given by law to one person to retain the property belonging to another until some claim has been satisfied.

Permitted hours: The period during which sale of alcoholic liquor is permitted to non-residents.

Personal representatives: The executors or administrators of a deceased person.

Petty sessional court: In England and Wales, the court of a petty sessional district, a magistrates' court, a court of summary jurisdiction, a police court.

Procurator-fiscal: In Scotland, the law officer who prosecutes in certain criminal cases at sheriff courts.

Proof spirit: Spirit which contains 50.76% of water against 49.29% of ethyl alcohol; another definition is: spirit which at a temperature of

51°F (10.5°C) weighs 12/13ths of an equal measure of distilled water. The strength of spirits is expressed as so many degrees over or under proof, e.g. 30° under proof means that the liquor contains 70% of proof spirit.

Sheriff court: In Scotland, although strictly an inferior court, it has extensive civil and criminal jurisdiction, and some administrative functions. The administrative officer is known as the sheriff-clerk.

Slander: Defamatory words spoken of a person which results in that person suffering damage, this damage having to be proved to the satisfaction of the court.

Truck Acts: A number of Acts passed during the last century and still in force, designed to stop the 'truck system', that is paying wages otherwise than in cash; the system had involved the issue of tokens exchangeable for goods.

Young person: A person not under 14 but who is under 18 years of age.

Appendix I

HOTEL PROPRIETORS ACT, 1956

An Act to amend the law relating to inns and innkeepers.

1. *Inns and innkeepers*

(1) An hotel within the meaning of this Act shall, and any other establishment shall not, be deemed to be an inn; and the duties, liabilities and rights which immediately before the commencement of this Act attached to an innkeeper as such shall, subject to the provisions of this Act, attach to the proprietor of such an hotel and shall not attach to any other person.

(2) The proprietor of an hotel shall, as an innkeeper, be under the like liability, if any, to make good to any guest of his any damage to property brought to the hotel as he would be under to make good the loss thereof.

(3) In this Act, the expression 'hotel' means an establishment held out by the proprietor as offering food, drink and, if so required, sleeping accommodation, without special contract, to any traveller presenting himself who appears able and willing to pay a reasonable sum for the services and facilities provided and who is in a fit state to be received.

2. *Modifications of liabilities and rights of innkeepers as such*

(1) Without prejudice to any other liability incurred by him with respect to any property brought to the hotel, the proprietor of an hotel shall not be liable as an innkeeper to make good to any traveller any loss of or damage to such property except where:

(*a*) At the time of the loss or damage sleeping accommodation at the hotel had been engaged for the traveller; and

(*b*) The loss or damage occurred during the period commencing with the midnight immediately preceding, and ending with the midnight immediately following, a period for which the traveller was a guest at the hotel and entitled to use the accommodation so engaged.

(2) Without prejudice to any other liability or right of his with respect thereto, the proprietor of an hotel shall not as an innkeeper be liable to make good to any guest of his any loss of or damage to, or have any lien on, any vehicle or any property left therein, or any horse or other live animal or its harness or other equipment.

(3) Where the proprietor of an hotel is liable as an innkeeper to make good the loss of or any damage to property brought to the hotel, his liability to any one guest shall not exceed fifty pounds in respect of any one article, or one hundred pounds in the aggregate, except where:

(*a*) The property was stolen, lost or damaged through the default, neglect or wilful act of the proprietor or some servant of his; or

(*b*) The property was deposited by or on behalf of the guest expressly for safe custody with the proprietor or some servant of his authorised, or appearing to be authorised, for the purpose, and, if so required by the proprietor or that servant, in a container fastened or sealed by the depositor; or

(*c*) At a time after the guest had arrived at the hotel, either the property in question was offered for deposit as aforesaid and the proprietor or his servant refused to receive it, or the guest or some other guest acting on his behalf wished so to offer the property in question but, through the default of the proprietor or a servant of his, was unable to do so;

Provided that the proprietor shall not be entitled to the protection of this subsection unless, at the time when the property in question was brought to the hotel, a copy of the notice set out in the Schedule to this Act printed in plain type was conspicuously displayed in a place where it could conveniently be read by his guests at or near the reception office or desk, or where there is no reception office or desk at or near the main entrance to the hotel.

3. *Short title, repeal, extent and commencement*

(1) This Act may be cited as the Hotel Proprietors Act, 1956.

(2) The Innkeepers' Liability Act, 1863, is hereby repealed.

(3) This Act shall not extend to Northern Ireland.

(4) This Act shall come into operation on the first day of January, nineteen hundred and fifty-seven.

SCHEDULE

Notice

Loss of or Damage to Guests' Property

Under the Hotel Proprietors Act, 1956, an hotel proprietor may in certain circumstances be liable to make good any loss of or damage to a guest's property even though it was not due to any fault of the proprietor or staff of the hotel.

This liability however:

(a) Extends only to the property of guests who have engaged sleeping accommodation at the hotel;

(b) Is limited to £50 for any one article and a total of £100 in the case of any one guest, except in the case of property which has been deposited, or offered for deposit, for safe custody;

(c) Does not cover motor-cars or other vehicles of any kind or any property left in them, or horses or other live animals.

This notice does not constitute an admission either that the Act applies to this hotel or that liability thereunder attaches to the proprietor of this hotel in any particular case.

Appendix II

IMMIGRATION

The Immigration (Hotel Records) Order, 1972

3. This Order shall apply in the case of any hotel or other premises, whether furnished or unfurnished, where lodging or sleeping accommodation is provided for reward, not being premises certified by the chief officer of police of the area in which they are situate to be occupied for the purposes of a school, hospital, club or other institution or association.

4. (1) Every person of or over the age of 16 years who stays at any premises to which this Order applies shall, on arriving at the premises, inform the keeper of the premises of his full name and nationality.

(2) Every such person who is an alien shall also:

(*a*) On arriving at the premises, inform the keeper of the premises of the number and place of issue of his passport, certificate of registration or other document establishing his identity and nationality; and

(*b*) On or before his departure from the premises, inform the keeper of the premises of his next destination and, if it is known to him, his full address there.

5. *The keeper of any premises to which this Order applies shall:*

(*a*) Require all persons of or over the age of 16 years who stay at the premises to comply with their obligations under the foregoing Article; and

(*b*) Keep for a period of at least 12 months a record in writing of the date of arrival of every such person and of all information given to him by any such person in pursuance of the foregoing Article;

and every record shall at all times be open for inspection by any constable or by any person authorised by the Secretary of State.

Explanatory Note: The provision made corresponds to that in Article 19 of the Aliens Order, 1953, as amended (in 1957), which ceases to have effect on the coming into operation of the Act of 1971 (1st January 1973).

Appendix III

UNDERSTANDING A WAGES ORDER

The Order of widest application in this industry, and incidentally the most complex, is the Licensed Residential Establishment and Licensed Restaurant Order (LR) and this has been chosen to illustrate an employer's obligations. Other Orders differ in detail. The basic principles of LR Orders are:

1. Normal working week—40 hours, excluding recognised meal breaks; one day counts as a weekly day of rest.

2. Employees are classified in 10 groups of ordinary workers and 4 groups of service workers; lower rates apply to those under 21 in groups 1, 10, 11, 12 and 13—workers in other groups must by definition be 21 or over. Managers and assistant managers are excluded.

3. Minimum weekly wages are specified according to the location of the premises—London, rest of the country.

4. Hourly deductions (maximum 40) are allowed where the employer makes available (i) full board and lodging seven days a week, and (ii) meals while on duty to non-resident staff.

5. Service workers with a guarantee agreement may be paid at a reduced rate, subject to their receiving a certain minimum income from gratuities.

6. Extra payments are due for—

> Overtime—which, by agreement, may be spread over a fortnight.
>
> Sunday work.
>
> Night work—reduced intervals for rest.
>
> Work on a rest day, unless another day off is given within 10 weeks.
>
> Customary holiday—double time if worked; if not, single time.
>
> Spreadover—split duty beginning and ending more than

12 hours apart on the same day or continuation into next day (14 hours in premises with up to 35 bedrooms); exceptions for seasonal establishments.

Laundry, uniform, protective clothing, where cost not borne by the employer.

Temporary transfer to higher grade work.

7. Holiday entitlement—accrues week by week so that annual holiday is based on length of service; holiday to be taken within holiday season, with extension for workers in seasonal establishments. When employment terminates, some accrued holiday remuneration may be payable.

Advice to Employers:

Check weekly minimum rate applicable to each employee according to job group, and whether he lives in or out. Keep records of time worked, ascertain total hours worked each week and calculate wages due on the basis of the Order even if a higher overall payment has been agreed, making sure that all extras have been included.

INDEX

Absence from duty, 47
A.C.A.S., 43
Accidents, to guests, 34; to staff, 42
Accommodation, hotel proprietor's duty to provide, 16
Accounts, payment by guests, 22, 36
Advertisements, control by planning authority, 126
Alcoholic liquor, 137
Alterations to licensed premises, 84
Amusements with prizes, 120
Animals at hotels, 18

Bailment, 18, 23, 137
Bar, children in, 101, 111; definition, 137; young persons employment, 100, 110
Beer, definition, 137
Beerhouse licence, old, 86
Betting and Gaming, 119
Billiards, 117
Boarding house, 21
Bookings, hotel, advance, 24; by agent, 26; for a party, 26; cancelled, 26
Business, purchase and sale, 121; one-man, 122; partnership, 122; company, 123; insurance, 131
Business Names registration, 122
Butter, 72
Bye-laws (Scotland), 109

Cafés, wages order, 61
Cancelled bookings, 26
Cars, on hotel premises, 18
Cash shortages, 50
Cheques, acceptance of, 36
Children, 101, 137
Clerk to the justices, 137
Company, limited liability, 123
Compensation, redundant licence, 90; tenant refused renewal of lease, 130; tenant for improvement, 130
Consumption of liquor, 97, 109

Contract, accommodation, 24; business transfer, 121; definition, 137; employment, 41, 45, 51
Copyright music, 118
County court, 137
Court of session, 137
Cream, 72
Credit, sale of liquor, 100, 111
Credit cards, 36
Crown courts, 138

Damage, to guests' property, 18; by guests, 32; by laundry, 134
Dancing—see Music and dancing
Death, of guests, 31; of employer, 55; of licence-holder, 88, 107
Deed, 138
Deposit, on reservation, 24; for safe custody, 18
Disabled persons, 66
Disciplinary procedures, 50
Disclaimer notice, 19, 23
Dismissal of staff, 51, 54
Discrimination, guests, 22; employees, 44
Divorce evidence, 29
Drinking-up time, 97, 109

Employee's duties, 42
Employer's obligations, 42
Engagement of staff, 44
Entertainment licence, 104
Extended hours order, 96

Fire precautions, 34, 66
Food, control of premises, 75; hygiene, 73; provision by hotel proprietor, 16; standards, 71
Fully-licensed premises, 138

Gaming, 119
General order of exemption, 94
Gratuities, 60
Guest, at an hotel, 15; at a private

INDEX

hotel, 21; difficult, 30; registration, 29; terms and conditions, 28; see also Property
Guest house, 21

Health and safety in employment, 46
Hire purchase, 133
Hotel, definition, 15, 138, 141; private, 21
Hotel Proprietors Act, 141
Hygiene, 73

Ice cream, 73
Improvement by tenant, 130
Industrial Tribunal, 54
Infectious illness, guest, 30; staff handling food, 74
Inn—see Hotel
Insanity of guest, 30
Insurance, business, 131

Justices licence, 80

Kitchen waste, 76

Labour relations, 43
Landlord and tenant, 129, 138
Late night refreshment house, 118
Laundry, 134
Letters for guests, 32
Libel, 138
Licence, types of, 79, 104
Licence-holder, display of name, 92; entertainment of friends and staff, 98; residence on premises, 93, 109
Licensed non-residential establishment, 61
Licensed premises, alterations, 84; conduct of, 92, 108; winter closing, 98
Licensed residential establishment, 62
Lien on guest's property, 19, 138
Liquor, sale of, 98, 110
Local Authorities, powers, 128
Local Veto (Scotland) 104
Loss of guest's property, 17

Managers, employment of, 57
Maternity leave, 48
Measure, sale of liquor by, 99, 102
Milk, 71
Misrepresentation, 27
Music and dancing licence. 117

Negligence, guests' property, 19; in employment, 52
Notice, in employment, 51

Occasional licence, 89, 107
Occupier's liability, 34
Offices, Shops and Railway Premises Act, 65
Off-licence, 80, 104
On-licence, old, 81

Performing right, 118
Permitted hours, 93, 108, 138; exceptions, 97, 109; off-sales, 98, 108; registered clubs, 105
Personnel management, 43
Pests, damage by, 76
Petty sessional court, 138
Phonographic Performance Ltd., 118
Planning, 126
Police, licensed premises, 101, 111; registered clubs, 116
Private hotel, 21
Procurator-fiscal, 138
Proof spirit, 138
Property, guests', 17, 31
Protection order, 88
Provisional grant of a licence, 84, 106
Public Health Acts, 128
Public house licence (Scotland), 104
Purchases, 133

Race Relations, 35
Redundancy, 53
References, 56
Refreshment house, late night, 118
Refreshment licence (Scotland), 104
Refuse collection, 129

INDEX

Registered letters for guests, 32
Registration, business names, 122; club, 113; company, 124; guests, 29, 145
Removal of licence, 89
Renewal of licence, 85, 106
Representative occupation, 57
Reservations, hotel—see Bookings
Residential licence, 80
Residents in hotels, 29; sale of liquor to, 97
Restaurant, customer's property, 23
Restaurant licence, 80, 104
Restricted hotel licence, 104
Restriction order, 109

Safe custody of guests' property, 19
Safety of guests and customers, 34; of staff, 46
Sanitary conveniences, 128
Seasonal licence, 83
Service charge, 28, 60
Sex Discrimination Act, 44
Sheriff court, 139
Shops Act, 59, 62, 127
Six-day licence, 83
Slander, 139
Smoking, by staff handling food, 74
Special hours certificate, 96
Special order of exemption, 94
Structure of premises, control by justices 84; by licensing board, 104

Suicide, 31
Supper hour certificate, 95

Tobacco, 119
Town and country planning—see Planning
Trade Descriptions Act, 35
Trade unions, 43
Transfer of licence, 87, 107
Traveller, 15
Tribunals, 54
Truck Acts, 49, 139

Unfair Contract Terms Act, 19, 23, 133
Unfair dismissal, 54
Unlicensed hotel, consumption of liquor, 104
Unlicensed place of refreshment, 61

Wages, deductions from, 49; during illness, 47; itemised statement, 50; payment by cheque, 50
Wages Councils Act, 60
Wales, Sunday permitted hours, 94
Water, 128
Weights and measures, sale of liquor 99, 112

Young persons, employment, 63; sale of liquor to, 99, 110; sale of tobacco to, 119

KD 2517 .H6 B8 1979
Bull, Frank Joseph, 1898-
Hotel and catering law